10 Steps for Parenting Your Grieving Children

Anne Hatcher Berenberg, Ph.D.,
Vicki Scalzitti, and Jack Cain

10 Steps for Parenting Your Grieving Children

Copyright © 2011 Anne Hatcher Berenberg

Published by:

AVJ Publishing

info@grieving-children.com

ISBN: 978-0-578-08748-1

Library of Congress Control Number: 2011911198

Printed in the United States of America

Book Design: Deborah Perdue

www.illuminationgraphics.com

Cover photograph by Jack Cain

1. Children and Death. 2. Grief in Children. 3. Parenting Grief

CONTENTS

Preface . . . .*i*

Introduction . . . .*iii*

10 Steps for Parenting Your Grieving Children

A framework for thinking about your children's grief......1

Step 1: Let Grief Happen 3

First reactions; talking about the death to children of different ages; funerals—should children go and how can you prepare; children need to tell their story; children's grief takes many forms; important messages to give children; letting your own grief happen

Step 2: Start to Cope with Aloneness 27

Keeping children from feeling isolated; marshalling resources, including those at school; preventing the "loss" of surviving parent—how to manage day by day

Step 3: Time to Move On...
Taking Some Control over Grief 33

Ways to take some control over grief; being present to your children now; dealing with misbehavior

Step 4. Examine the Past 37

Not getting stuck in the past; preserving good memories and good family connections; what if the person who died was a difficult person; misperceptions and guilt

Step 5. Examine the Future 45

Dealing with your own worries about the future; tools for anxious children; relaxation techniques; hopes and dreams; reunion fantasies

Step 6. Examine the Present 55

Appreciating the positives; encouraging resilience; developing talents and interests

Step 7. Practice 59

Fostering growth; carving out time for each child; family "gratefulness" exercises

Step 8. Crowd Out Negatives 63
Exercising physically and mentally; getting rid of "all or nothing"
thinking; reinforcing resilience; designated "worry time"; dealing
with anger

Step 9. Do Unto Others 71
Healing by reaching out and giving to others

Step 10. See This as a Lifelong Process 73
A life-changing process; reworking loss and grief at different
developmental stages

Additional information about special circumstances:

Parenting Children Who Are
Grieving the Loss of a Sibling.....................77

Parenting Children Who Have Lost a Friend
or Loved One to Suicide 93

Parenting Children Who Have Experienced
Multiple Losses 103

Parenting Children Whose Friend or Loved One
Was Killed by Another Person 117

A Few Words about Trauma 137

Afterword 147

Appendix A: A Story about Anxiety—
Managing It Step by Step 149

Appendix B: A Story about Many Small Losses
Adding Up to a Big Burden 155

References 158

Acknowledgements 161

PREFACE

This book is drawn from our experiences, both personal and professional.

Anne and her sons lost their wonderful daddy to a heart attack when Daniel was nine and Tommy was a month shy of his fifth birthday. Within the next four years, they experienced two more deaths. First, the boys' beloved grandmother died. A few months later, a woman with a gun entered Tommy's elementary school, killing the boys' friend and neighbor Nicky and grievously wounding several other children.

Vicki, her husband Bill, and her son Billy lost his cherished little brother Joey in a tragic accidental drowning when Billy was eight.

Jack and his daughter Nicole lost her brother Adam to suicide, her mother to cancer, and her sister Stephanie to congestive heart failure in a twenty-month period before and just after her own son's birth.

We have parented through the worst of times and know they do not last forever. We treasure our adult children.

We know from our professional work as well that children can grieve deeply and still grow up to become people who are living happy, productive lives. In Anne's practice as a clinical psychologist, she has worked with many children, adolescents, and their parents dealing with the loss of someone very important to them. Vicki has helped hundreds of bereaved children and families as Manager of Children's Bereavement Services and Coordinator of the Good Mourning Program for Children, Teens and Families at Rainbow Hospice & Palliative Care in Mount Prospect, Illinois. We have learned from all of our clients and are grateful to each one of them for letting us into their lives.

The stories found in italics throughout this book are drawn from the lives of real children and real parents. Of course, names and details have been changed, and sometimes stories have been consolidated, but all are based on the experiences of people like you and the grieving children you care about.

INTRODUCTION

You are a parent or someone who loves, cares for, and is involved in raising a grieving child. You have lost someone that you and your child or children love. Perhaps they have lost their other parent, their sibling, a grandparent, other relative, or a friend. You yourself are grieving. If you have a spouse or partner, he or she is experiencing grief also. Or you are coping with single parenting, perhaps for the first time, in addition to dealing with grief. Yet you know you have to help your children.

This outline gives you a roadmap of what you can do. There are 10 Steps you can follow to deal with the challenges you are now facing as a parent or a person in a parenting role.[1]

Many parents and caregivers will get all the information they need from the main section of this book. If you are parenting children who have lost a loved adult to an illness or to most kinds of accidents, the main section is likely to be enough.

After the main text of this book, there are sections giving additional information about dealing with special circumstances:

- the loss of a sibling

- the loss of a loved one to suicide

- multiple losses

[1] These 10 Steps have been adapted especially for children from the 10 Steps found in *Now: Overcoming Crushing Grief by Living in the Present* by J. Cain and A. Berenberg, which are appropriate for adults.

- when a loved one is killed by another person, including in a car crash

- a few words about trauma

If any of these special circumstances apply to you and your children, read the appropriate section or sections. They are written for you about the children you care for. Most people will find it helpful to read the main text first, then turn to the extra section(s) that relate to their special circumstance(s). You may want to flip back and forth between the main text and a special section, particularly when you are trying to figure out what to say to your children about the death. Whatever works best for you is the way to use this book.

A note to professionals—counselors and therapists, facilitators, physicians, physician assistants, nurses, clergy, and educators:

While this book is written for parents and caregivers, you will find the ideas in it to be very useful as you are helping grieving children and those parenting them find their footing in their changed worlds. The sections on special circumstances will be especially helpful. This book is a resource for all who counsel bereaved children and/or their parents. And it is for teachers, too. Teachers are very important people in their students' lives. They can make a crucial difference to children who have suffered losses.

10 Steps for Parenting Your Grieving Children

A framework for thinking about your children's grief

- The goal is to support your children in their natural healing.

- You are working through your own grief at the same time as you are helping your children.

- You may be afraid that your children have been or will be damaged by their loss and bereavement.

- Children process what has happened and is happening according to their own developmental level. A small child, a school age child, and a teenager will all understand and experience the death of an important person differently—and that will change for each one of them over time.

- Children's grief looks different from adult grief.

- Children will need to re-work their understanding of death and/or loss again at each developmental level. Expect this to happen.

Step 1:

LET GRIEF HAPPEN

Emma and Sammy were in the family room watching a television special when their daddy came home late from work. He said hello to them, then had a late supper with their mother, Laura. When the show was over, 5-year-old Sammy could hardly keep his eyes open. His dad carried him up to bed, sang him snatches of their favorite lullaby, and tucked him in. Ten-year-old Emma came upstairs on her own. Her dad happily agreed to read a chapter in a book with her before she went to sleep.

The next morning Emma woke up, got dressed, and went downstairs for breakfast. She was startled to see a friend of her mother's sitting at the kitchen table. "What are you doing here?" asked Emma. "Better ask your mom," the friend replied. Laura took a deep breath. She sat with Emma, put an arm around her, and said, "Daddy died last night." "You mean <u>your</u> daddy," said Emma urgently. "No, I mean <u>your</u> daddy." Laura's voice broke.

Emma asked, "How could that happen?" Laura said, "His heart stopped beating and he died. It's called a heart attack." "Why didn't anybody save him?" Emma cried.

Laura decided not to tell Emma every detail of the rescue attempts by the EMTs, the nightmarish trip in the ambulance to the hospital, the final giving up of hope. She knew that Emma was trying to get her mind around something that seemed incomprehensible to Laura, too. She tried to stick to the essentials.

"I called 911 when Daddy said he was having pain in his chest. His chest hurt because his heart wasn't beating right. The paramedics took him in the ambulance to the hospital, but they couldn't keep his heart beating and the doctors couldn't, either. If your heart doesn't beat, your body can't keep on living." Laura and Emma began sobbing together and hugged each other. That was all Emma wanted to know right then. Soon she announced that she was hungry and really needed her breakfast.

In the very beginning...

You will need to tell your child or children about the death using words and concepts tailored to each individual child.

• It is important that you—or another trusted adult who knows the child well—be the one to tell him or her what has happened, rather than having the child learn from picking up bits and snatches of adult conversation or hear from an unreliable source or sense your tension and not know why. You want your child to get accurate information, to feel that he or she can ask questions, and that you can be trusted to tell the truth.

• For all children, it is important to use the word *died* rather than a euphemism like "went to sleep," "passed on," or "left us" because these can be misunderstood and lead to both confusion and anxiety.

• Give your child the basic information, then follow his or her lead. Many children don't want to or are unable to digest too much information all at once. Answer questions as they come along. Know that you may have to answer some questions more than once and that the questions may not make sense to you but do have meaning to a child.

For very young children...

Laura could hear Sammy stirring upstairs. She ran up so that she could catch him alone in his room, as the house was gradually filling up with people When she told him that his father had died, Sammy put his fingers in his ears and turned his face to the wall. He shrugged Laura off when she tried to hug him. Finally, she went downstairs. Later, Sammy appeared in the kitchen, marched up to her friend and demanded to see Daddy. Laura's friend said that he had died. Sammy asked, "Well, when is he coming back?" Laura joined the conversation and told Sammy that Daddy's heart had stopped beating and that meant he couldn't breathe, or move, or feel any more. Sammy went to play but soon came back, saying that when Daddy came home from work, he needed to help Sammy with his Legos. Laura gently said that Daddy wouldn't be coming home again, but she would help. Sammy shouted that she was no good at Legos and he'd wait for Daddy. Later that evening, after she had once again told Sammy that Daddy was dead and wasn't going to come walking in the door, she heard him asking her sister and her friends the same questions he had asked Laura: "Can Daddy go peepee? Can Daddy ride his bike? When will Daddy sing to me again?"

- Little children need to be told in very simple terms that death means that the person's body is no longer alive: their loved one can no longer breathe, move, or talk. The person who died can no longer feel pain or be sad. And the child won't see that person any more.

• Most very young children will not be able to grasp the idea of *being* and *not being*. They do not have the concept of irreversibility.

• Be ready for many concrete questions. You can be very specific that the deceased cannot eat any more, go to the bathroom any more, etc. And don't be surprised when the little child to whom just yesterday you carefully explained that Grandpa has died asks, "When is Grandpa coming to see us again?"

• Expect them to ask the same questions many times, not because they haven't been listening or are trying to push your buttons, but because their brains are not developed enough to "get it." Answering their repeated questions again and again in the same way, instead of trying to explain differently, actually aids their understanding.

• If it fits with your family's belief system, you can illustrate the idea that the body dies but the soul or spirit lives on by putting your hand into a glove. Wiggle your fingers. This is like a person who is alive. Take your hand out and distance it from the glove. The glove no longer moves; it is like a dead body. But the hand is still moving in another place, just as the soul or spirit is still there. It just isn't in the body anymore, just as the hand isn't in the glove anymore.

For children between about 5 and 8...

• Somewhere between ages 5 and 8, most children will be able to conceptualize and understand death as the end of biological functioning—life. You talk in the simple, concrete terms mentioned above, but they start to "get it" in a way their younger siblings cannot (or they could not when they were younger).

• Be ready to answer questions. Get as much information as you need to tell your child what actually happened in this particular death and why it happened at this particular time. Then give the child as much information as he or she asks for, but no more than is requested.

▶ For example: "Her heart wasn't working right. It stopped beating. The doctors couldn't get it started again. People can't live if their hearts don't beat."

▶ Or: "He was driving really fast and couldn't stop the car when the truck in front of him stopped. His car crashed into the truck." Child: "Why did he die?" Your answer: "His chest was crushed and he couldn't breathe any more. And then he died."

Laura was able to talk to Sammy quietly one night at bedtime and tell him that Daddy's body was dead but his spirit lived on. It was like the wind. Sammy couldn't see it or touch it, but he could feel it and know that it was there. Sammy came to love putting his face to the open window to feel the breeze because it reminded him of Daddy.

• Most children of this age are now able to get the idea (as Sammy did) that the spirit or soul lives on but is like the wind, something you can't see or touch, but that you can feel and know is present. If this fits with your family's belief system, it can be a comforting concept for a child.

• Children of this age can understand the idea that the person they loved lives on in their memories. The memories they have of their loved one are theirs to keep, like a gift they have received which belongs to them. This idea can be embraced by families of any belief system.

For children of about 7 or 8 and older (including adolescents)...

Over the course of the next few days, Emma asked more questions about heart attacks and what happened. Laura dealt with one question at a time, answering as best she knew. It was painful, but Laura was glad Emma felt able to come to her with her concerns. Emma also wanted to know who would coach her soccer team now that Daddy couldn't and whether they were going to have to move. Laura said the assistant coach would take over and they would definitely stay in the same house until the end of the school year; she'd let Emma know what they'd do after that when there was time to figure it out.

• From about age 7 to 8 and older, children and adolescents will have concerns about their own lives and futures and how the death will affect them. The conversations may be less about the way the body stops working and more about how this loss will affect their lives. These issues are discussed in the sections that follow.

• Children of this age, especially adolescents, may have questions about how or why death occurs. They may want to talk about meaning.

▶ You don't have to have all the answers. Your job is to be a sounding board for them to figure out answers that have meaning for them at this stage of their lives—or to connect them with other adults, such as a clergyperson, a caring adult friend or relative, or a counselor who has the time and interest to grapple with the big questions about the meaning of life and death.

Laura was exhausted. The visit by the minister to discuss the funeral service had been comforting and wrenching at the same time. It took what felt like her last ounce of strength to go to the funeral home with her sister and her husband's sister to choose a casket, figure out an announcement and make plans for the funeral. When she got home, she collapsed in a chair, only to be pounced on by Sammy wanting her to fix a broken toy, then saying he wanted Daddy to do it. She told her sister that it would just be too much to take Sammy to the funeral. He could never sit quietly for that long. Besides, he was so little. He wouldn't understand what was going on anyway. Her sister told her that it would be really important to take Sammy. He needed a concrete way to say "Good-bye" to his Daddy to help it seem real and give him some sense of finality. She offered to be "assigned" to Sammy the day of the funeral, ready to answer his questions and tend to his needs so that Laura could focus on her own grieving. Laura gratefully accepted.

It is important for most children to go to the funeral or memorial service of their loved one.

- This helps the grieving process by making the death real, marking its finality, and providing a before and after reference point. The funeral or memorial service provides a meaningful ritual to express feelings, linking the bereaved family to the community, and bringing in religious faith, if it fits your family's beliefs. These rituals are ways in which you and your children can say good-bye to the person who died.

- Children who are shielded from this important symbolic and community event often feel less grounded and even cheated, robbed of an important way of working through the death and saying good-bye. The good intentions of those who feel they are protecting the children end up backfiring.

The next day, Laura sat down with both children and told them what to expect the day of the funeral. She told them that Daddy's body would be in a casket, described the mourner's room and who they would see there, said that Daddy's favorite hymn would be sung, and that people would say things about Daddy. She told them that some of the people would cry and that was OK. Others wouldn't, and that was OK, too. She said there might be times when it seemed like a big party of people getting together to tell nice things about Daddy and it was OK to smile and laugh as they remembered him.

• Prepare each child for what to expect at the planned ceremonies and events as they apply: the wake or viewing, if there is one; the funeral or memorial service; the funeral procession and burial, if those will happen; any reception or luncheon, sitting shiva for Jewish families.

Emma announced that they needed to have yellow roses at the funeral because they were Daddy's favorite, and Laura immediately agreed. Emma also had many questions about what Daddy would wear. Laura let her choose the tie, a task that Emma took very seriously. Laura watched as Emma laid out all the possibilities, picked one, then changed her mind and picked another. Emma also wanted to put a Sudoku book that Daddy had been working on in the casket. Laura explained that this could go in as a way for Emma to show how well she knew Daddy and what he liked; of course, Daddy couldn't do Sudoku anymore now that he was dead. Emma asked if she could make some drawings to go in the casket. Laura encouraged her to do so, as an expression of her love for Daddy. Sammy chose to put in a Lego construction he'd made, then insisted he wanted to give his favorite teddy bear to Daddy.

• Plan for each child's participation in the funeral or memorial service.

▶ If you have a very young child (or an older child with a short attention span), ask another adult to come with you to the funeral and take primary responsibility for that child. This person can give the child whatever attention he or she needs, answering questions as necessary. (Or, if the child becomes too restless to stay through the whole service, the designated adult can quietly take the child out.) You should be able to focus your attention on the funeral and your own needs at that time.

▶ Children can place a letter, drawing or toy in the casket prior to the funeral to express their love for the person who died. If that's not in keeping with your religious tradition or you simply don't feel comfortable with putting anything into the casket, you can have a special place at home where the child places these tokens. When there has been cremation, drawings or letters can be buried with or kept near the urn, or they can be scattered with the ashes.

▶ Older children may be able to have some voice in planning the funeral, memorial service, wake, or reception. This can range from suggesting the loved one's favorite hymn or psalm, to helping choose photos to be displayed at the funeral home, to telling what kind of cookies must be on the table later at a reception or at shiva.

▶ Adolescents may wish to speak at the service or to write words that someone else will deliver, but they should not be pressured to do so.

• Often, it is helpful to arrange for a private viewing at the funeral home for the children.

Laura made special arrangements with the funeral home for her and the children to view the body privately and put the treasures in the casket before the funeral. She asked her sister to come with her for support. When they got there, Sammy pulled at her hand to go see Daddy, but Emma hung back, saying she wanted to remember Daddy the way he'd been when he was alive. Laura didn't pressure Emma, letting her stay outside with her aunt while Laura and Sammy saw the body. Sammy marched right up and put his fingers under Daddy's nose. Finally, he pronounced that Daddy wasn't breathing anymore. Laura realized how important it was for him to find this out for himself rather than just hear it from grown-ups. As they put the pictures, the Sudoku, the Legos and the teddy bear into the casket, Laura said to Sammy that Daddy had loved Sammy very much and knew that Sammy loved him very much. But Daddy wouldn't have wanted Sammy to bury anything with his body that Sammy really needed himself. Sammy could remember Daddy each time he hugged the teddy bear. With that reassurance, Sammy was able to take the teddy bear back into his own arms.

• Some children, particularly younger ones, may wish to touch the body to know that the person is no longer breathing and able to move. This isn't disrespectful. It's just a way of making the abstract idea of death real to them.

• If your child says that he or she doesn't want to go to the funeral, take some time to see what this is about before deciding what to do.

When Laura and Sammy came out after viewing Daddy's body, Emma suddenly said she didn't want to go to the funeral after all. Laura's first impulse was to tell her she didn't have to do anything she didn't want to do. But Laura worried that Emma would always regret not being there for the ceremony. So she took Emma to a quiet spot and asked her why she didn't want to go. After awhile, Emma was able to say that she was afraid she'd have to look in the casket. Laura reassured her that the casket would be closed during the funeral. She could participate in the service by listening to what people said about Daddy, saying the prayers, looking at the beautiful flowers, and singing the hymn. Relieved, Emma joined the family.

▶ Sometimes children are anxious about something that you can help them understand better or can change to make them more comfortable. If they have fears that you can reassure them about, they may be able to attend.

▶ Sometimes children pick up on your worry about their ability to last through the service and say they don't want to go. This is the time to reassure them (and you) that there will be someone there specifically to be with them and help them with what they need.

▶ Some children still are absolutely adamant that they don't want to go to the funeral or wake, no matter how well you listen to their concerns and reassure them. Then it is time to make alternative arrangements for them to stay home without anyone feeling ashamed about that choice. It defeats the purpose of the "Good-bye" if the child is dragged kicking and screaming to the funeral.

• If for some reason your child is not able to go to a funeral or memorial service for the person who died, plan a private ceremony of some kind at a later time during which the child can say a ritualized good-bye.

> ▶ This could involve suggesting the child to write or draw something, then lighting a candle and dedicating it to the loved one who died,

> ▶ Or burying the child's letter or picture in a special spot, perhaps under a new planting,

> ▶ Or creating some other ritual that suits your family and in which the child can participate.

Children need to be able to tell their story.

• At first, the most important thing is for each of your children to forge an age-appropriate narrative or story about their special person's death. This narrative will probably include:

> ▶ Some explanation of the illness (if applicable)

> ▶ The child's understanding of the death itself

▸ The child's perceptions of what happened after the death (probably including the funeral and the people who comforted them)

▸ How the child felt at various points (and feels now).

On a Monday evening during a local bereavement program, the children in a group for 4-year-olds were each sharing the story of what happened to the important person in his or her life who died. After several children told about the car accident or illness that caused the death of their important person—Mom or Dad or brother or sister—it was Jack's turn. Jack said simply, "A spider bit Baby Josh and he died."

The group facilitators knew that Jack's brother had died from SIDS – Sudden Infant Death Syndrome. So they told Jack's mother, Lisa, what he had shared and suggested that she make sure Jack understood what had happened to his little brother.

Lisa talked with Jack and he listened very attentively to her explanation. "Baby Josh," she said, "didn't wake up one morning and when I went to check on him, he wasn't breathing. His body had stopped working and he had died. That is why we don't have him here with us anymore and why we can't see him." She asked Jack if he understood.

Jack sighed and looked at his mother. "Was Baby Josh sick?" he asked. "No," said Lisa. "Did he get hurt?" asked Jack. Lisa assured Jack that Joshua had not been sick or hurt – he had just died. Jack became increasingly anxious during the conversation, lying across the kitchen chair, rocking on his tummy, his gaze focused on the kitchen floor. Josh looked up at Lisa, with wet eyes. "That," he said to his mom, "isn't a story."

For Jack, the idea that his baby brother could be here one day and gone the next without anything apparently happening was *incomprehensible on even the most basic level. It was not what he (and all bereaved children) needed – a cohesive, understandable, age-appropriate way of describing what happened to the important person who died. It was also very frightening to think that anyone could just drop dead at any time. After talking with the facilitators at their bereavement program, Lisa went back to Jack and began a new discussion of what had happened to Baby Joshua, telling him the story he'd needed all along.*

She explained that Joshua had gotten very sick, very fast during the night. Before Mom found out that he was very sick, Joshua had stopped breathing, his body stopped working, and he died. That sickness, she explained, was called SIDS. Jack listened carefully and asked if he could get sick like that. Lisa explained that only little babies get that kind of sickness and most babies don't get that sickness at all.

From then on, Jack could tell his story about his brother Joshua and about SIDS –- the "sickness that only little babies get"—that Joshua got and died from. The spider, no longer necessary, disappeared from Jack's story entirely.

- Parents and caregivers can help their children tell their stories in whatever way suits each child best. It's also OK if another trusted adult talks, writes, plays or draws with the child.

  ▶ Even though you gave an initial explanation to your child right after the death and answered immediate questions, your child's need to create his or her own narrative continues.

  ▶ Encourage your child to use his or her own words. When you talk with your child and continue to answer questions, be sure to use words the child can understand.

▶ It often helps to have the child's story written down. For young children, this will be a collaborative effort with an adult. Older children and adolescents may want to do this on their own. Very little children may need to play out their stories using dolls or other toys.

▶ Your children may want or need to draw pictures. Some children will want to illustrate the stories. Some will want to draw pictures to show their feelings. Some will want the whole story to be done in pictures.

▶ This narrative will need to be re-worked at different developmental stages. What worked for the child when he or she was 4 will no longer be sufficient when he or she is 9, and that story, in turn, is likely to be inadequate for a 15-year-old.

  − This may or may not be a physical re-writing of a written story.

  − It may just be a re-thinking using new conceptual tools and a new capacity to make use of information.

▶ If you have more than one child, each one will have a different story and a different way of expressing it.

• Sometime after this narrative about the loved one's death has been established, your child will want and need to have a story about his or her special person's life.

  ▶ The time for this life story may come within days of getting the narrative of the death straight or it may come weeks or months later. The story of the loved one's life will certainly be one to be revisited and added to over time. (We'll talk about positive memories again in a later section.)

▶ For now, it's enough to know that this story will include:
  – Memories of the special person and what they did together when that person was alive

  – Perhaps the child's continuing relationship to the person who died (as a role model or as the one who showed him/her how to play a game, for example).

▶ Just as with the narrative about the important person's death, you can help each child find his or her own best way of telling about and recording the memories of that person's life: writing, drawing, telling you the story while you write it down, playing it out are a few possibilities. Remember that each child has his or her own timetable for this and his or her own favorite modes of expression.

As you go on after the first days...

Laura put a sandwich on Sammy's plate.

"This is peanut butter and strawberry jam. You made it wrong! I hate strawberry!" Sammy shouted.

"You liked strawberry jam yesterday."

"I don't like strawberry now. I won't eat it."

Laura sighed and made Sammy a peanut butter and grape jelly sandwich.

"This is yucky. You never give me what I want."

"What's wrong with it? It's peanut butter and grape." Laura felt exasperated and hurt. She was trying so hard. Why was Sammy rejecting her best efforts?

"You cut it into four pieces. I want it in two pieces. You never do anything right! Nothing is right!" Sammy howled.

Laura started to angrily snatch up the plate, ready to tell Sammy that his lunch was over, when she caught herself up short. Instead, she crouched by Sammy's chair and gave him a hug. *"I know, Sammy. Nothing seems quite right now because Daddy is dead and can't be with us. We all wish that he could be here making sandwiches with us. I can't make that happen. But I will always love you and I will take care of you. Even if I'm not as good at peanut butter and jelly sandwiches as he was."*

Children's grief can take many forms.

• Anger, irritability, and frustration are common, often in fairly frequent short bursts.

▶ Your child feels a need to make things as they used to be and is frustrated and irritable when they can't be.

– Identifying what things can stay the same ("Friday night can still be pizza night; the family still goes to church"), and what things have changed ("Daddy can't drive us to church anymore and sit next to us in the pew") can be clarifying and reassuring.

– Honest recognition that the world your family has known really has changed and that this is hard for all of you can help to define this as shared pain—you're in this together.

▸ For younger children particularly, the anger or irritability may be directed toward you, the surviving parent. The child feels it is the parent's job to make the world seem right and it just doesn't.

▸ Often, the child focuses on little things that aren't right. If you, the parent, get hung up on those little things (which aren't really the issue), it can lead to frustration all around because there will always be another thing at another time.

— Recognize this for what it is: making a vague sense of the world not being right into something concrete.

— If you take this personally, it can feel very hurtful. But if you can say to yourself that your child is signaling you how wrong the world feels right now, you can see that it's not really about you.

— Then you can focus on giving your child a hug, empathizing with his or her sense of dislocation, and reassuring your child that you all will get through this

▸ Older children may be angry with God, the doctors, or the person who died. Let them know you understand their sense that something happened which made the world feel wrong, focusing on the feeling without buying into the blaming.

• Some children are sad.

• Some children are morose, down on themselves.

• Some see themselves as victims.

• Some children feel no hope.

• Some children may feel guilty because they think that something they did caused the death. Those children will need repeated reassurance that this is not so.

• Some may feel guilty because they may have been mad at the person who died.

• Some no longer trust the world to be a safe or fair place. This can spill out in their attitude toward you, authorities, institutions or religion.

• Children may show their grief and stress by being exhausted, lethargic, hyperactive, or having problems with focus, attention, concentration, and memory. Understand that these are symptoms of grief/stress just as much as tears are.

• In general, young children are more concrete in their worries, needs, and understanding, whereas adolescents often need to grapple with the bigger issues of life and death.

If you have more than one child, expect them each to respond differently to this death. They are of different ages, different temperaments, and have had different life experiences. They have had different relationships with the person who died, so they will be mourning different losses.

The waves of grief—in whatever form—are different for children.
   • Adults often experience crashing waves of grief that almost sweep them off their feet and may last a long time, or powerful rage that stays with them. Children, however, usually experience feeling states that are more like choppy water, with smaller, shorter bursts of emotion. They are often able to play and have fun in between periods of sadness, anger, or irritability. This doesn't mean they aren't grieving.

   • While grief affects children at many different times of the day, it often shows up very strongly at bedtime. Although it slows down the getting-to-sleep process, it is often worth giving the bit of extra time and attention that are required to respond to your child and to comfort him or her.

> ▸ It can feel hard to do because you are tired and want to be wrapping up the day, but your availability when your child is most needy and receptive makes a big difference.

> ▸ Build this extra time into your bedtime routine if you find that it is needed. If you start the process of getting ready for bed earlier, it won't end up keeping both your child and you up too late.

Your grief also needs to happen, and in ways that do not overwhelm the children.

   • Your children are likely to notice that you are sad, as well as more spacey and/or irritable than usual. Agree with them. It's true. Label it as grief so that it is understandable. You all are grieving and you all show it at times. Part of loving together is grieving together. But try not to completely fall apart frequently in front of the children.

▶ Getting teary or crying now and then in front of them and with them is OK and perfectly normal.

▶ Uncontrolled sobbing, ranting, or getting hysterical is best done out of your children's view and perhaps with another adult for support. It can be very frightening for children to see.

▶ Even if you don't feel strong at the moment, you can reassure the children that you and they will get through this, and in so doing find some reserves of strength in yourselves.

Three key messages you give to your children are:

- "I am sad but OK."

- "It won't always be this sad."

- "I can still take care of you."

Your children need you to be the parent. They should not feel responsible for taking care of your grief, even though you are really hurting.

• Some children feel they now have to be the caretaker or take on the role of the parent who died, becoming pseudo-mature or the "good child."

• Sometimes it feels easy or even good to let that happen, but taking on too mature a role too soon actually gets in the way of the kind of growth that leaves a child feeling strong and solid.

• Your task may be complicated by well-meaning relatives who tell your child "You're the man of the house now" or "Since Daddy has you for a daughter, he still has a little woman to take care of him." You can tell them kindly but firmly that you think your child is wonderful and responsible, but you aren't expecting him or her to take on an adult role.

Mornings were rough for Laura. She found herself almost overwhelmed by grief and loneliness as she bustled around, helping the children get ready for school. She thought she would burst with the pressure of the tears welling up in her eyes.

On one of the early days, Laura had completely broken down sobbing over breakfast. Emma raced to get her tissues and tea, while Sammy put his head in her lap and said, "Don't cry, Mommy." When she continued to sob, Sammy sounded frightened and his pleas for her to stop crying became ever more urgent. Emma started to seem older than her years, trying to clean up the kitchen and pack Sammy's backpack. Laura was deeply touched, but she knew this wasn't something that should be a daily occurrence—a feeling that was reinforced when she got a concerned email from Emma's teacher that afternoon saying Emma seemed withdrawn and preoccupied.

So Laura made arrangements with her friend Joan. If she thought she was going to "lose it," she'd call Joan and they would arrange for an emergency hug. They would meet in one of their driveways for 10 minutes after they'd gotten the children off to school. Laura would spend the whole time sobbing and Joan would simply hold her. Then they would both go on with their days. But knowing she could call Joan and be held was enough to help Laura hang on through the morning. And Laura made plans for regular visits with her sister just to talk, as well.

At the same time, find other avenues for pouring out your own grief.

- Talk about your grief, pain, and confusion with close friends or family members who are receptive, to a grief counselor or therapist, or to a clergyperson.

- Having several different people that you can talk to and cry with gives you the support you deserve and helps you to stay in your parenting role with your children.

- If you don't have family and friends who can support you, seek out a support group at your local hospice or bereavement center, try an online group such as www.opentohope.org or www.griefnet.org, and/or start by keeping a journal.

Prioritize how to spend your energy during the early stages of your own mourning, putting the children at the top of your list. Figure out how you can give each child some real attention each day while also taking care of yourself.

Step 2:

START TO COPE WITH ALONENESS

In a bereavement group for 7- to 9- year-olds, the children were sharing thoughts about life without a parent. One child mentioned that his dad wasn't there to shoot hoops with anymore. Another talked about missing her daddy's familiar coat and big shoes that had always greeted her at the back door — so many changes, little and big, in the lives of bereaved children.

One 8-year-old girl, Melissa, began to talk softly about the loss of her mother. She talked about seeing a friend of hers at a shopping center. The friend was going through racks of clothes at a sidewalk sale. The friend was with her mom. Melissa sighed and looked down at the floor. Then she looked up and said, "It's different too — with just a dad. Some people think, like for sleepovers — that it's different without a lady there." Melissa was already encountering some of the random and unexpected changes in the life of a bereaved child, realizing how complicated even the simplest social interactions and opportunities can become.

At the end of the meeting, the facilitators asked Melissa if they could talk to her dad about the sleepover issue. Melissa said that she wanted to think about it first. The next week, Melissa told the facilitator that she talked to her dad and he said that Melissa could have her friends sleep over with her at her aunt's home. This solution worked on many levels—alleviating any discomfort or anxiety that other parents may have felt, allowing Melissa to participate and reciprocate, providing some important "girl time" for Melissa with her aunt, and allowing Melissa's aunt to get involved in providing opportunities and support for her.

Aloneness for children means feeling isolated from others rather than literally being alone in the house. Making and/or maintaining social contacts is often more complicated than it was in the past.

Swiftly marshal resources to keep children from becoming isolated.

• Other children may be afraid that they will "catch" the death of a parent or sibling from the bereaved child. (Your child may worry about this, too. If so, clarify for your child that this doesn't happen.) Generally speaking, this is less of an issue with the death of a grandparent.

• Work with school personnel (principal, social worker or counselor, teachers) to tell classmates and other children who are important to your bereaved child about the death in a way that promotes their reaching out to your child, encouraging them to think of ways they can connect with your child, as well as giving them an opportunity to hear about the death in a way they can understand and to ask questions. If you are working with a grief counselor or a therapist, that professional may be helpful in working with the school.

• If friends and relatives ask you what they can do, encourage them to invite your child over, take your child places, be available as an adult mentor, or make it OK for their own children to play with your bereaved child. They can include your child when they go on family or parent-child outings to the park, ice rink, beach, or the ice cream parlor.

• Encourage family members to support each other at this stressful time. This includes the extended family. The child needs the love and support of all.

▶ You can be a model by treating other family members with the love and understanding that you would like them to show you.

▶ This is particularly important if the person who died had complicated relationships with others, perhaps due to problems with alcohol, drugs, or mental illness. It is also very important if death was complicated and confusing, such as death in an automobile accident when he or she was at fault, death from a preventable or treatable disease, violent death, or even death after a long and torturous illness.

▶ If you feel very worried about how your family is coping with the stresses and changes associated with your loss, seek help from a professional specializing in working with families in grief. Many hospices offer services to bereaved children and adults, even if they did not use hospice during the course of their loved one's final months or days.

Help your child identify sources of support.

• These supports should include both adults and children, family and friends, and may include professionals (in-school or out-of-school).

• Encourage your children to have play dates and continue with established group activities or sports. Find a way to clue in coaches and group leaders about the child's loss.

• Bereavement groups designed for children offer opportunities for children to be with peers who have had the same experiences. To find a center for grieving children near you, use the Internet to find www.dougy.org—it lists resources by area. Your local hospice or teaching hospital may offer assistance or a program nearby.

The most painful loss for many children is the "loss" of the surviving parent. You understandably have been preoccupied if your loved one has been ill. If the death was sudden, you are coping with the shock. Now you are grieving. In all of these circumstances, it is difficult to be truly available to your surviving child or children.

• Reach out to get support for yourself so that you have the capacity to be present to the children. Plus, you deserve it as a mourner in your own right. Your support can come from friends, family, grief counseling or other therapy, support groups (including on-line support groups), or stress-reduction classes such as yoga.

• Be sure that there is some time each day when each child has your full attention and involvement. (Just being in the same room while texting on your cell phone, working at your computer, or similarly multi-tasking doesn't fill this need.)

• Figure out how to draw in extended family and/or friends to carry out some of the functions that you cannot always perform—someone to roughhouse with the kids the way Daddy used to, someone to take a child to piano lessons and admire progress made, for example.

• Re-establish the nuclear family as a viable unit; you are still a family and can see yourselves as a strong, loving one.

• Re-establish appropriate rules and expectations for the children. Children feel more comfortable knowing that the parent or parent-figure is in control and that there are limits on their behavior.

• You can and should develop a life beyond that with the children—and allow the children to have one separate from you. Take time to do things with adult friends. If that feels overwhelming, start small. Get yourself through the morning, then the afternoon, and then the evening. Take a little time each day to do something that you can do for yourself, a project or activity that doesn't revolve around the person who died. It could be reading a book that isn't grief-related, going for a run, trying a new recipe, planting a flower, getting back in touch with an old hobby or experimenting with a new one...it doesn't need to be something big.

Step 3:

TIME TO MOVE ON... STARTING TO HAVE SOME CONTROL OVER GRIEF

You feel grief and know it must be honored, yet you know it's not helpful to be breaking down all of the time in front of the children. While you know that it is OK to cry occasionally, you are trying to keep those breakdowns from being frequent and uncontrolled.

- You can set up "appointments for grieving." Set aside a time and place that can be like a sacred moment to devote yourself to grieving. Then honor those appointments. When a wave of grief hits you at a time when you do not feel comfortable immersing yourself in it, such as in the middle of your child's soccer game or when you're at work, remind yourself of your appointment time, or make a new one closer to the moment so that you can carry on now.

- A quick relief is "shower crying," taking a few moments out of view and earshot of the children to let out pent-up emotions, then pulling it back together when rejoining the children.

Start seeing yourself and your children not as victims, but as survivors. You are getting through this together.

It is important for you to be present to your children *right now* **for what they are doing** *right now* **and what they are interested in** *right now*. Bereaved parents often see their children and everything the children do through the lenses of their bereavement. Also see them as the children you have always loved, unique individuals who continue to grow and learn.

 • This means enjoying their interests and accomplishments, listening to their concerns. Really valuing them for who they are, letting them know they are important in and of themselves, is one of the most important things you can do for them.

 • Some flexibility in routine or rules after the upheaval of the recent death is appropriate and relevant. The children may need extra cuddling, fewer new challenges, more time for bedtime stories at night, or smaller meals for a while.

Some parents of teenagers were talking in a parents' group about how difficult it can be to know how to respond to their bereaved children. How far, they wondered, do you let a kid go? How do you know whether the bad grades, smart mouth, slamming doors, or eye-rolling are just adolescent behaviors or whether they are irritability associated with grief? Several parents admitted that they themselves could be cross and short-tempered at times, especially since their loss, and they really appreciated it when friends, family, and colleagues were understanding with them. They wanted to be at least as responsive and understanding with their children as they hoped others would be with them. But a question kept surfacing throughout the discussion: How do you know whether the main issue is grief, which you want to be sensitive about, or whether it is inappropriate behavior, which you might need to address?

Finally, one mother who had been involved with the group the longest said, "You know, after all the back and forth, this is what I've figured out. Whether or not it's grief, some things just have to stop. If what is going on is harmful or hurtful, if it has the potential to cause on-going problems, or if the behavior is becoming increasingly difficult for the parent or the kid himself to manage, it's time to address it."

However, it is also important to recognize that bereaved children can misbehave. Inappropriate behavior, such as hitting or saying hurtful things to others, is still inappropriate. You can empathize with your child's pain while still setting firm limits on inappropriate behavior. "I know you're upset, but it is never OK to hit." Or "Sometimes when you feel sad, you want to hurt someone, but let's put those sad feelings into words so you won't feel like you need to hit."

• Remember that your child has a life beyond his or her bereavement. Any individual upset may or may not be directly related to the bereavement, though the response may be more intense because your child is already stressed.

  ▶ Your child may be unhappy about something that happened at school or in the neighborhood that he/she would have been unhappy about anyway. Your child can be helped to deal with the school or neighborhood issue in an appropriate fashion.

▶ Sometimes you need to say to your child something like, "I know you're sad about Daddy dying, but I think you're crying now because your sister has a play date and you don't. When you stop crying, we'll figure out what you can do this afternoon."

▶ Sometimes your child will engage in simple misbehavior or testing. Then the child needs to be corrected and/or have an appropriate consequence that has previously been established for this behavior. This is reassuring because it shows your child that the ground rules of his or her life have not been taken away.

　　– For example, if the rule is no electronics in bed and the consequence for breaking that rule is that the item be taken away for the next day, that rule and that consequence still holds true.

　　– You can couple the consequence with an extra hug and warm reassurance that you know he or she will remember the rule tomorrow.

Step 4:

EXAMINE THE PAST

Parents often assume that the sad events in their children's past will **determine the future.** But children are much more than the sum of their painful experiences. Their natural tendency is to move forward and grow. Your job is to let this happen.

Most often, it is we, the adults, who become stuck in the painful past.[1] Sometimes we may need help to see that we must not let our preoccupation with the past keep our children stuck.[2] If you feel you can't get out of the past, you can reach out for help from a grief counselor, mental health professional, or hospice program.

Some children may get stuck on what they feel is a betrayal by the person who died: "She told me she was going to beat the cancer and she didn't!" or "He told me he'd never leave me!" Hear them out, then introduce the alternative explanation that this was a wish made out of love rather than a promise that was broken. If this is something you can't work through with your child, either because he or she is too stuck or because it's just too

---

[2] You can look at the Examine the Past section in the book *Now: Overcoming Crushing Grief by Living in the Present* by J. Cain and A. Berenberg for ways an adult can deal with this step.

hard for you to deal with, it may be helpful to connect your child with a caring professional.

It helps your children when you help them find times in their own history when they were strong and resilient. This will help them build a life-story and a self-image of themselves as someone who can cope with the stresses of life. "Tell me about a time when..." Or "I remember when you..."

For children, the most important issue often is holding onto their memories of the important person who died rather than being stuck in the past. They need to be helped to develop an enduring sense of whose child they are. This is particularly important for children who have lost a parent.

It was a long drive to the children's paternal grandparents' house in a neighboring state and Laura dreaded coping with all the trucks that shared the highway. But she knew her in-laws loved the children and Emma and Sammy were clamoring to go. When she saw them melt into their grandparents' arms, she knew the effort was worth it. The children soaked up the love and attention of their grandparents and of the other relatives who gathered. Stories were told about their father, including how he'd had a temper as a little boy, just like Sammy, and how he always sneezed in series of three, like Emma. Everyone felt rejuvenated after the weekend and they made plans to get together on a regular basis.

• Continued connections with people related to them through the parent who died— grandparents, aunts, uncles, and cousins—give children a sense of continuity and belonging. They remain their parent's child even after that parent has died. They have a shared history.

• This kind of connection is a wonderful source of memories.

• And it enriches the lives of all concerned, including the bereaved adults.

Emma started collecting her favorite "Daddy things," beginning with some children's books from his old room at his parents' house. With a little help from Laura, she created a "memory box" that included the old baseball cap he always wore when he coached soccer, his cologne, his famous chili recipe, a map he'd drawn on a napkin to give Laura directions one day, and numerous photos, which Emma carefully labeled. Meanwhile, Laura sat Sammy on her lap and asked him to tell her what he remembered about Daddy. She typed his snatches of memories into the computer—helping Daddy wash the car, Daddy's scratchy beard, the lullaby Daddy sang at night. These recollections could belong to Sammy in later years even as his memory of his father began to fade and meld with stories he had been told about his father by others.

Help your children find the best way for them to remember their loved one who died.

• They can write or dictate what they remember about their loved one, especially what they did together.

• They can help pick out photos and cherished items as mementos they keep. They may want belongings of their loved one that never would have occurred to you or the other adults around them, so it is important that they be involved in the choice of keepsakes. They can find or design a special box to keep these mementos in—a memory box.

• Children and adolescents who are savvy with computers and other electronic devices may want to use them to save music they associate with their friend or loved one; to create a power point presentation, a slide show, or a video about their important person; to use their own creativity to devise an electronic memorial that has meaning to them.

• They can be a part of rituals that you establish with them to remember the loved one, such as lighting a candle on the anniversary of the loved one's death. They may have their own ideas about what should be part of any family rituals, and you can find a way to incorporate those ideas if possible.

Children need to have an image of their loved one in their minds that they can live with. For most children, this image of the person who died can and should be predominantly positive but not unrealistic.

• The loved one can and should be mentioned in conversation when it is natural to do so. He or she is an important part of your child's life and history. You can remember together that this was Grandpa's favorite song or laugh over the way your child's sister who died used to insist on wearing the same hat every time she went outside. Making mention of the loved one who died off limits gets in the way of your child finding a healing and healthy place for that important person in your child's life story.

• It is also important to talk about how the loved one felt about the child: "When you were born, Daddy couldn't wait to hold you." "Grandma loved reading with you."

- If the child had a generally positive relationship with the person who died, it's helpful to nurture the happy memories and identifications. It's strengthening for your child to know that Daddy would have been proud of his daughter's learning to ride a bike or that Mommy had a good ear for languages just like her son.

- But it isn't helpful to re-create the person who died as some kind of a saint. It can be a relief to the child to laugh over Daddy's grouchiness when he was tired from work or to know it is OK to have been angry with him for missing the soccer game.

The more disabled Matt's father became from multiple sclerosis, the worse his temper got, and the harder it became for Matt to visit him in his assisted living facility. His dad grumbled the whole time Matt was there, complaining about how seldom he came, how little time he spent, and how he knew that Matt did not want to be there. Like a lot of self-fulfilling prophecies, it was certainly coming true, as Matt became more resentful and reluctant to see his dad. Dad called Matt selfish and self-centered and taunted him about how glad Matt would be when Dad had died and he didn't have to bother coming anymore. One particularly hurtful thing that Dad said repeatedly was that he knew Matt couldn't wait to forget him.

Matt kept asking his mom why he had to go, as Dad did not seem to enjoy his visits anyway and it was tough getting there since Mom and Dad were divorced. His mom felt strongly that he should continue to see his dad. She kept it simple as she explained her reasoning to him.

"Matt, this is your chance to be a better son to your dad than he can be father to you. Do you remember any of the stories about you and Dad when you were a little boy—back before he got sick? Dad

was so proud of having a son. He loved spending time with you and you enjoyed being with him, too."

Matt chimed in with some happy old memories, then said, "But he's not like that any more. I don't like to go see him now."

"I know how frustrating it is to be with Dad now," his mother replied. "It's hard to be with him, so it's only natural that sometimes you'd rather stay away. He isn't being fair to you when he says you're selfish. His illness has gotten the better of him. The person he is now is all that is left of that devoted Daddy." Matt's face softened. His mother continued, "And Dad wasn't wrong when he said that he will die soon. It probably won't be all that long before he dies. I think it would be better not to have regrets." The regular visits continued.

When Matt's mom got the call that his dad was in the hospital and that the time remaining was very short, she took Matt to the hospital. Dad was already unresponsive. Matt stood awkwardly at the bedside, asking if he could just go. A wonderful nurse suggested that he read some Bible passages that his dad had asked a chaplain to read to him a couple of days earlier. "Your dad," she said, "will still be able to hear you." So Matt sat at the bedside and read the passages. A few minutes later, the nurse brought a basin of water and asked Matt to wipe Dad's face. Over the next few hours she showed Matt how to moisten Dad's lips and helped him rub cream on his hands. He combed Dad's hair and found Dad's favorite oldies station on the radio. Mom and Matt shared stories – good and bad, funny and painful. They even laughed over how stubborn and difficult Dad could be at times, Matt often shaking his head with tears in his eyes.

In a few hours, Dad's life came to its natural end.

If the person who died was a very difficult person, someone who may have caused the child or others pain, this needs to be worked through instead of left to fester under the surface. You need to feel that it is an OK subject for your child to discuss with you and appropriate others, such as a trusted relative, a grief counselor or other mental health professional, or in a children's grief group.

• It is not disloyal to talk about the hard aspects of living with that person. Your child can understand that Mommy had a bad temper and made big mistakes when she drank too much. Or that Daddy was so sad that he never had fun with his children and sometimes said mean things.

In the weeks following his father's death, Matt's mom enrolled him in a bereavement program for children. He was resistant. "I'm not that sad," he would say. His mother, however, persevered, believing as she always had, that it isn't always the most loved folks who are the hardest to grieve and that complicated relationships can have long-term ramifications in the lives of children.

In his last year of high school, Matt attended his fifth memorial service, provided by the children and families bereavement program he had attended. After Matt lit a memorial candle in honor of his dad, he walked up to one of the facilitators and gave him a hug. "My dad," he said, "always said I'd forget him. And I never have. He was my dad, good or bad, and I'll remember him always."

• And your child can also be helped to know that no one is all bad, and if we think about it we can find some things about the person that were nice or that the child loved. Your child can remember both the bad and the good.

• For children who have lost a parent or sibling with many flaws, it is important for you to know—and to help your child know—that each child is a separate individual who is not doomed to follow in the footsteps of the one who died. That is true even if the child in some way reminds others of the dead parent or sibling, whether in looks, gender, or temperament.

• It is also important for them to know that their having been angry at the person who died because he/she was mean, irritable, neglectful or any other reason did not cause the death of that person. And they do not need to feel guilty about sometimes having wished that the person was dead or gone. The child's wishes and feelings didn't make the person die.

Some children may have misconceptions about their loved one's illness or death. It is important to clear those up and help your child to know the actual facts. Then your child will be able to have an accurate story to hold on to.

• Some children (and many adults) have the idea that they could have prevented the death if only they had done something different—or even felt differently about the loved one. You may need to help bring out these feelings of responsibility and guilt, either in your child or in yourself or both.

• Then you can help your child let this idea go—and let it go yourself. Sometimes this involves recognizing that we all wish we had more power and control than we actually do.

Step 5:

EXAMINE THE FUTURE

Brian glanced at his watch, then called upstairs to his daughter. "Come on, Jane, brush your hair and get ready. The school bus will come in just a few minutes." "I hate brushing my hair," came her reply. "You want to look nice for school," he cajoled. "I don't care. It's too hard," Jane retorted as she rushed past her dad on the way out, her hair still messy. And her choice of clothes! Brian almost stopped her at the door to make her change either her shirt or her skirt—they didn't go well together at all. If only her mother were still alive…She would know how to get Jane to look good every morning without a squabble.

As he sat, imagining that Jane would grow up to be a social outcast because she'd never learn to do her hair or dress nicely, his phone rang. It was Toni, the mother of Jane's best friend Chloe, calling to confirm that the girls would be coming to her house after school. Brian found himself blurting out his fears to Toni. "She sounds just like Chloe and half of the other girls in second grade," responded this experienced mother. "You should have seen the outfit Chloe put on this morning! Nothing went together. But they'll all learn by doing. They look at each other and talk together. You'll see that by next year they do a much better job." "What about the hair?" asked Brian.

"They all want long hair and they all have trouble brushing it. I'll give the girls some tips this afternoon, then, when you come to pick Jane up, I'll ask her to show you what she's learned. And we'll keep practicing each time she comes over." Brian thanked her, paused, then gulped out his deeper worry. "Do the other girls like Jane? Do you think she is going to be OK?" "Yes, she fits in well with a nice group of girls, including my daughter. You're a rock for her. And she's been reaching out to the women in her life—like me, like her teacher, like her Brownie leader, like her grandmother. I think she's doing well."

Brian relaxed a little as he headed off to work.

It is important to identify and deal with your own worries about the future, recognizing what is exaggerated or unrealistic. Any of us, adult or child, feels anxious when we are facing a situation that seems threatening to us, but don't feel competent to deal with. Our job is to use our best judgment to realistically assess the threat (usually moving the threat level downward) and our ability to manage the situation (usually realizing that we are more competent than we initially felt we were).

- Parents often leap to the conclusion that their children will be forever scarred by their experience of loss.

  ▸ This need not be true; the children can instead become more resilient, stronger, more compassionate people.

  ▸ If you can focus on fostering the children's interests and strengths right now, and help the children see themselves as survivors who will continue to move forward, the children will continue to grow.

► We are all affected by every experience we have. That is what makes each of us unique.

• Learn to separate your own anxiety from that of the children. Learn not to read something dangerous into the normal ups and downs of childhood or adolescence or into the normal anxieties of those stages of life.

► If you find this difficult to do on your own, seek help from an experienced parent who knows about children of this age, your child's teacher, school social worker or counselor, a mental health professional, or resources from your local children's grief center.

It is normal for children to have some increase in anxiety after a loss. If it doesn't last more than a few months and doesn't interfere with their daily functioning, you can just give a little extra reassurance and hugs. If it continues, grows more pronounced, and/or if the child craves more and more reassurance, it's time to help him or her deal with it more actively.

If children exhibit unrealistic fears or marked anxiety of their own, give them tools to manage anxiety. (See Appendix A if you would like to read a story that gives you a script showing how one family helped their child through anxiety following a death.)

• Give your child some basic information about anxiety. Do this at a time when you are both feeling relaxed and calm. This can be in the form of a story, using language that fits the age and developmental level of your child. It's important that you talk to your child in a warm, caring way that presents you as partners in dealing with his/her anxiety, and that the child doesn't feel shamed in any way.

- The key concepts are:

  ▶ There is a part of our brain—we can call it *Mr. Worry*—that reacts immediately to anything that seems like it could be dangerous before the thinking parts of our brain can evaluate whether or not there really is a threat.

  ▶ This fast-acting part of our brain often makes mistakes, exaggerating and over-generalizing the threat while underestimating our capacity to cope.

  ▶ *Mr. Worry* sends out signals to our bodies that can make our heart beat faster; get us to take quick, shallow breaths; slow down our digestive system (making us feel "butterflies" in our stomachs or have stomachaches); make our throats dry and our palms sweaty. (This is often called the "fight or flight" response.)

    – When our bodies feel like that, we start to think there must be something really big to be afraid of, even when *Mr. Worry* is wrong and there isn't.

    – If we run away from a situation when we first feel the physical symptoms of anxiety, we'll never find out that they go down gradually after about 10-15 minutes.

▶ We need to slow down and give our good thinking brains time to figure out whether there really is something to be afraid of and how we are going to manage the situation.

• See if your child has any misconceptions that you can clear up with factual information. As we've noted, children often are confused about the facts of someone's death. For example, a child may feel that he can catch his mother's heart attack by having been near her, or, conversely, that she had a heart attack because he was away from home. But simply having the right facts, while necessary, often is not enough to put a stop to the brain's "fast-forward" to fear when the *Mr. Worry* area is triggered by a situation, sight, sound, or smell that it associates with a threat.

• Help your child pare big worries down into smaller, manageable ones. Concentrate on what is doable now.

▶ Usually you can break things down into a series of small steps. For a child who is afraid to be away from home, this could be gradually working up to an overnight stay at a friend's house by ever-longer play dates, then an overnight at your house.

▶ Build on many small successes in situations that gently stretch his or her comfort level. Don't put your child in a situation that is genuinely too much and will lead to failure.

• Support your child in walking *through* anxiety.

▸ The anxiety level will come down naturally if you don't feed the flames or run away from it.

▸ Don't reinforce avoidance as a way of coping with anxiety by rescuing your child at the height of anxiety. This validates his or her fears. Instead, help your child gain mastery from living through it.

• In moments of high anxiety, don't just reassure your child. This won't stick and he or she will just beg for more reassurance soon. Instead, help your child work through why *Mr. Worry* got it wrong.

▸ First, tell your child that you see he or she is feeling really worried, scared, or upset (choose the word that fits best) in a warm, caring way.

▸ Second, identify what is happening—*Mr. Worry* is talking and trying to get your child to think this is a catastrophe.

▸ Then, encourage your child to dispute *Mr. Worry's* conclusions and tell *Mr. Worry* how he is wrong. Help your child identify how *Mr. Worry* is confused or is exaggerating and over-generalizing the danger and underestimating your child's capacity to cope.

▸ Help your child bring down the physiological symptoms of stress through the deep breathing and relaxation exercises outlined in the next section. Do this before talking back to *Mr. Worry* if your child is extremely tense.

▶ Now your child will be ready to think about what he or she wants to do, rather than listening to that distorting *Mr. Worry*. Help your child focus on what he or she can actively do.

• If your child's anxiety is long-lasting and crippling, keeping him or her from resuming normal activities or having happy moments for months, seek professional help.

(Many of these strategies are Anne's adaptations of those set forth in greater detail by T. Chansky in *Freeing Your Child From Anxiety*[3]. See that book for discussion of what Dr. Chansky calls the "worry brain" and how to deal with it.)

Parents can do relaxation techniques with children. These techniques are useful generally, and can help you as you help your children. In addition, sometimes it is an important early step in managing an acute moment of anxiety to relax the body and mind before attempting any analysis or problem solving.

• One technique is to breathe slowly and deeply from the diaphragm. Start out by lying next to each other on the floor on your stomachs—that forces you to breathe correctly. Help your child think of soothing words that work for him or her, such as "I am safe," or "I can do it," or " God is with me." Put your hand on your child's back and say half of the words while the child is breathing in, then the other half as he or she is breathing out. Ask him or her to think the words as you say them.

• Many children like a technique that one of this book's authors (Anne) calls **Rainbow Relax.**

[3] See especially chapters 4 and 5, pp.56-100.

▶ Have the child tighten his/her feet and toes, then let them go, imagining them glow purple as they relax. Comment warmly on his/her relaxed purple feet and toes.

▶ Next tighten and release the legs, having them glow blue. Say that the child now has relaxed purple feet and relaxed blue legs.

▶ Then tighten the tush (let your child pick the word used for his/her bottom), and as it relaxes, it glows green. Review that he or she now has relaxed purple feet, relaxed blue legs, and a relaxed green tush.

▶ Do the stomach, then chest and shoulders, then arms and hands, and finally the neck and face, tightening and relaxing each set of muscles in turn, then giving it a color. Use some of the child's favorite colors. After each round of tightening and relaxation, review in order all of the relaxed colored body parts that you have done so far.

▶ End with the face glowing yellow. Do a final review of each glowing, relaxed body part in turn and talk in a soothing voice about how relaxed the child feels all over.

Encourage your children to have hopes and dreams. Don't worry if these may seem unrealistic. Part of the task of childhood is to try out ideas and to overreach sometimes. The main point is for the child to be thrusting forward, not to be stuck.

Some children may have fantasies about joining their loved one in heaven by dying themselves. Empathize with the child's longing for the missing person, but let the child know that he or she can keep the loved on in his/her heart while living life on earth. Be clear that this is what the important person who died would want him/her to do. Lovingly think together about the child's future on this earth. If belief in God and heaven is a part of your faith, you can emphasize that heaven is eternal and comes at the end of our God-given lives here; the loved one will wait until the child has had a full life.

Step 6:
EXAMINE THE PRESENT

In the painful and chaotic weeks following the death of Amanda, a young wife and mother, her husband Rich and their two boys, Andrew and Alex, struggled greatly with the challenges of everyday life. It seemed impossible that one human being could have accomplished all the things that needed doing every single day. The stress on Rich was eased just a little by the tremendous support the family received from their neighbors and community, particularly in providing meals. Most of the families they knew (and some they didn't) arranged a schedule of providing dinner for the family. Main courses and even delicious desserts arrived every night. But occasionally the boys remarked on missing one of Mom's favorite dishes, like her mac n' cheese. Sometimes they even got cranky about how something was made. Dinner time was a tough time for the boys even though there was good food on the table.

In a few weeks, however, despite the mad dash for the bus, the constant clean clothes shortage, and a dozen other daily crises, Rich began to notice that he and the boys were looking forward to some people's cooking very much. When Carol from next door made crab cakes, everyone seemed in a better mood. When Mrs. Bristi made spaghetti and meatballs, dinner conversation seemed slightly more upbeat. Alex once observed, with a mouth full of home-made brownies, that Mom hardly ever baked. She really didn't like baking. A few nights later, while they were enjoying Mom's friend Betsy's coconut cake, they were laughing and talking. Andrew blurted out, "You know, if Mom hadn't died, we'd never get this cake." The laughing stopped and all eyes turned on Andrew, who quickly looked down at the floor.

Rich took a deep breath and said, "Andrew, that's true. And I think that Mom would want us to be grateful for at least one thing today – for at least one thing that went right, even when so much stuff goes wrong. So, today, let's enjoy the coconut cake."

Andrew breathed a sigh of relief and the conversation resumed. Amanda's family had learned a first lesson in recovery and moving on. Find something to appreciate today. It won't change the difficult thing that has happened, but find something. And tomorrow, look for something else.

Encourage a family attitude of appreciation of the little things that are positive in life. You'll find them if you look. Notice the positives—even if they seem small in comparison with the tragedy you've been going through—in your children and in each child's actions.

What has a child done that is kind to another person?

What can you notice in a child's drawing that makes it creative?

Can you and the children notice the silly way the cat chases the ant on the floor?

Notice and encourage resilience in your children—and in yourself. You are all stronger than you think.[4]

---

[4] See T. Chansky, *Freeing Your Child From Negative Thinking* for many helpful ideas about fostering resilience, including a more detailed discussion of breaking problems down.

• In part, resilience comes when children (and adults) find that they can break down big problems into smaller, more manageable problems. Help your children see how something that seems overwhelming can be recast as a something they can cope with.

> ▶ For example, it's not that math is "impossible," as your child states; there is simply a hard math homework problem which someone can help the child figure out.

> ▶ Or, the room seems so messy that it feels like it can never be cleaned up. You can say, "Let's figure out a plan to first put the dirty clothes in the hamper, then put the books on the shelf, then the toys in the toy box, then straighten the bed."

> ▶ Or, your child is lonely today and feels like she or he will never have fun with friends again; but you can plan together for him or her to have a play date and put it on the calendar. In the meantime, he or she can do a Lego project or help you bake cookies.

• Comment on the times when your child overcomes obstacles, large or small, and encourage problem solving. And comment to yourself when you manage a difficult parenting situation. But also know it's normal for either you or your child to stumble sometimes. That happens. You just get back up again.

Help your children to discover their talents and interests. You can encourage your children to find what gives them satisfaction and then to follow those cues.

• These talents and interests can be used to work through grief. An artistic child can draw his/her feelings or remembrances. A child who likes to read can read books on grief—or on subjects in which he/she shared an interest with the loved one who died. A sports-minded child can hone the baseball skills begun by playing ball with Daddy. This should not be forced, however. It must seem right to the child.

• Whether or not your child uses his or her interests and talents to work through grief, finding them, trying them out, and choosing which ones to pursue are an important part of developing into a happy, competent person.

Step 7:

PRACTICE

When Emma asked to try out for the school play about six months after her father's death, Laura was surprised because her daughter had never been interested in acting before. Emma told her that her favorite teacher had suggested it. Laura was grateful that this teacher had her eye out for Emma, thinking of ways to bolster her up that wouldn't have occurred to Laura. She was pleased that Emma was expanding her horizons and continuing to grow.

Let your children try out new things and discover who they are. Make it safe to experiment.

Emma's play rehearsals meant one more carpool added to Sammy's life, though, and he complained loudly that Mom never had time for him. Laura felt like she spent a lot of time with Sammy, but when she really looked at it, she realized that while she was <u>around</u> Sammy a lot as they drove places or as she tried to cook dinner while checking her messages, she didn't actually spend that much time <u>with</u> Sammy. She told Sammy that every night at 7 p.m., while Emma did her half hour of reading for homework, she'd sit down on the floor with him and play for 20 minutes. They could *build with Legos, play with trucks, draw—anything they could do together. This was their special time.*

Laura kept to this as a firm commitment that Sammy could count on and she reminded him their special time was coming when he started to get out of sorts earlier in the day. Of course, she paid attention to him at other times, but knowing that he had his special time was something he could always hang on to. Somewhat to her surprise, Laura came to treasure this time, too. She let everything else go and just enjoyed these minutes with her son, marveling at how creative he was and how much fun they could have together when she wasn't worrying about everything else on her agenda. She loved hearing him laugh again and found herself laughing with him—a source of joy to them both.

Carve out some time each day when you can truly be present to each child. This means giving undivided attention, not just being in the same room while talking on the phone, checking Facebook, finishing up work from the office, or paying bills.

• It is important that you focus on that particular child: really be there, listening, attending to what the child is communicating.

• This time can be as short as 20 minutes each day, but it should be time the child can count on.

▶ For small children, this may be playing together rather than talking together.

▶ For older children, this might be doing a project together or just conversing about whatever the child wants to talk about.

Laura also made sure that she had 20 minutes of alone time with Emma as well. This came in the evening after Sammy was asleep. Laura sat on Emma's bed and they talked about whatever was on Emma's mind. Sometimes they talked about Daddy and sometimes they cried a little together, but often Laura could tell Emma how proud Daddy would have been of his daughter and all the new things she was doing.

Then Laura decided that she deserved 20 minutes with herself as well, and carved out time to do yoga each day.

The whole family can try having a sharing time for the positives of the day, perhaps over dinner, or this can be done with each child individually: "Let's be mindful about what is good, what we have, what we've done."

Try having a daily "gratefulness exercise"—one good thing about today. Sometimes it works well to do this as a family. Sometimes children need to do this one-on-one with a parent. Find what works best for you and your children, including what time is best.

Step 8:

CROWD OUT NEGATIVES

Olivia looked sullenly at her grandmother. "This really sucks."

Alice cringed. She hated hearing that language coming out of her 12- year-old granddaughter's mouth. But she was even more concerned by the negative moods Olivia got into after the death of her mother (Alice's daughter Liz). So she took some deep breaths to calm herself down, then decided to tune into what was most important. "What's wrong?" she asked.

"Nothing. Nothing at all," Olivia replied sarcastically. "Just that all my friends hate me, I always look horrible, and every teacher in my school is mean."

"Sounds pretty awful."

"It <u>is</u>." She glared at her grandmother. "You don't understand how hard it is."

Maybe I don't understand exactly what it's like for you, honey, but I know it's been tough. And right now, we need to dance." Alice put on a CD. Olivia looked skeptical and was starting to say something about her grandmother not listening to her kind of music when Alice took her hand and started moving to the music. "This was one of your mom's favorites," Alice told Olivia. Olivia nodded and soon was drawn into the beat. Together they danced until they fell onto the sofa, laughing and, in Alice's case, panting for breath.

"Not bad for an old lady!" giggled Olivia.

Doing something physical *and* doing something that stretches the mind each day are good for children as well as adults. This means limiting screen time (T.V., computer, video games, hand-helds, and smart phones) and monitoring content.

Alice made some iced tea. "You said all your friends hate you?" "Today, Tanya and Mia spent all of lunch just talking to each other and never looked at me. Then they went someplace together after school." "So you think that means they hate you?" asked Alice. "Well, they weren't paying attention to me." "And that's the same as hating you?" Alice wondered. "Well, maybe not. But I didn't like it." "I understand that you didn't like it. Does that happen every day?" "No." "So it could have been a one time thing, we don't know," said Alice thoughtfully. After Olivia nodded, her grandmother went on, "Did anyone pay attention to you today?" "Katie sat next to me at lunch." "Did you two just sit there not saying anything to each other?" "No, we talked about what people were wearing on our favorite TV shows and we looked at each other's nails." "Doesn't sound like Katie hates you." "No," agreed Olivia. "Would you like to ask Katie over after school sometime? You could ask her to bring her hairbrush, and you could pick out some nail polish, and you two could have an 'afternoon of beauty.'"

"Grandma, sometimes you have pretty good ideas."

Work to eliminate "all or nothing" thinking ("Nothing ever goes right for me!") and "always or never" thinking ("I never get a turn!") both in yourself and in your child. You can be clear that hard things are indeed hard. It's not useful to pretend that there aren't real challenges in all of your lives. But you and your children bring many strengths to life's challenges, there are some other people who care about you and them, and few things are happening now that are totally negative. Help introduce bits of flexibility into your and their thinking, noting the positive or neutral exceptions. [5]

A little later, Alice and Olivia had dinner together. The grandmother looped back to her granddaughter's other concerns. "So every teacher in your school is mean?" "Well," mumbled Olivia, "Mrs. Purdy isn't too bad, but Ms. Martin never smiles, and Mr. Small gave us so much homework. I'll never get it done." Her mumble turned into a wail.

"Let's talk about Mrs. Purdy first," said her grandmother calmly. "What are the things that are OK about her?" "She's nice to everybody and she lets everybody have a turn to talk," replied Olivia. "That sounds pretty good," noted Alice. "Yeah, I guess."

"What about Ms. Martin? Is there anything OK about her?" asked Alice. "Well," said Olivia thoughtfully, "She really knows what she's talking about." "So she doesn't smile much but you can learn a lot from her because she knows her subject?" "Yeah," responded Olivia, a trace of surprise in her voice. "I never thought science could be interesting before." "Sounds like she's too serious," Alice observed, "but not so bad because you can learn a lot from her." "Yeah," agreed Olivia.

Alice smiled. "Now let's look over your big assignment from Mr. Small together and see just what he's expecting you to do." "You don't know anything about this stuff, Grandma." "Not much, but you do. And I've had lots of practice reading directions and making big jobs into small ones. I bet we can break the assignment down into smaller pieces that you can manage."

---

[5] See T. Chansky, *Freeing Your Child From Negative Thinking* for more discussion of increasing flexibility of thought.

• A positive exception to all or nothing would be, "Did you notice that teacher's comment of 'Very good' on your paper? Does that match the idea that nothing ever goes right?"

• Or, for a neutral exception, "So you didn't get to play your favorite game in gym today, but you didn't have to play dodge ball, which you really don't like, either. Sounds like gym was OK, neither bad nor good."

Keep helping your child see his or her resilience when he or she manages to get through tough times.

After Olivia finished her homework, her grandmother told her how proud she was that Olivia got through something that had seemed so hard.

If a child is caught in negatives, it may help if you and that child set a designated worry time.

• Usually 10-15 minutes a day is about right. You can judge what works best for your child.

• Worries should be set aside until that time. Your child can write them down and put them in a special place until it's time to take them out, if that helps him or her to wait.

• During worry time, the child can worry to his or her heart's content. You should be there to listen to your child get his or her worries off of his chest.

• Then when worry time is over, it is time to focus on the positive present.

• After a while, your child is likely to discover that worries that seemed pressing early in the day were lessened or even resolved before worry time came around. You can rejoice with your child if this happens and use the left over worry time to talk about how resilient your child is and to simply have fun together.

See if your child benefits from a regular routine of relaxation techniques. From the time children are in grade school on up through high school, they usually can make good use of relaxation techniques, including deep breathing with calming words and progressive relaxation described in **Step 5**. These can be done together with you at bedtime or children can do them on their own at a time of their choosing. In any case, they can be available to your children as tools to use when stressed.

For some children, the most troublesome negative feeling is anger. It's fine for children have moments of appropriate anger from which they can calm down after the situation is resolved. But some children carry anger that pops out too strongly, too often, and/or at the wrong target.

• Remember that an angry child is a child who is feeling some kind of pain. When your child comes to you overflowing with anger, you can start by saying in a sympathetic way, "Unh, it looks like you hurt." This can soften the atmosphere and help the child see you as someone who cares about him/her.

• Your child may be carrying a load of unresolved anger from the death of his or her special person. If so, you empathize that the world doesn't seem right, while also helping the child gain some control when that anger starts to burst out in ways that get him or her off track.

▶ Usually, it helps children to have a chance to explore their angry feelings at a safe time and place. Sometimes, parents, grandparents, or others who love the child can do this at quiet times. For many children, it helps to talk to a counselor, either individually or in a group such as a children's grief group.

• You can teach your child how to keep anger from taking over in any given moment. Your child can:

▶ Take a step backward physically, breathe in slowly through his/her nose to the count of 1...2...3... then breathe out slowly through barely opened lips to the count of 1...2...3...4. (If the breath out comes out too fast in a big whoosh, have him/her breathe out through the nose.) Repeat. If necessary, suggest the child go into a different room to cool down.

▶ If possible, hugging a pillow, cushion, or folded up towel, crossing his/her arms over the pillow as he/she squeezes and breathes in 1...2...3..., then relaxing the arms as he/she breathes out 1...2...3...4, works even better to help a heated child calm down enough.

▶ Another way to go is to have the child do something very active but not aggressive to let out the anger energy. Shooting baskets, jumping rope, walking quickly—or, if the child must stay indoors—doing pushups against the wall or carrying something heavy, use muscles in a helpful way. Doing something aggressive like punching a punching bag doesn't work to defuse anger, so it actually doesn't help.

▸ Putting anger into words is an important step. Very angry children often need to start by cooling down or exercising off their rage before they can talk about it.

▸ Children who have more control can begin by using their words. Then they can move on to problem solving.

• Help your child figure out which techniques or combination of techniques work best for him or her.[6]

• Once these techniques have given your child a little room, work on enlarging the positive and neutral feelings as discussed above.

[6] See *What to Do When Your Temper Flares* by D. Huebner for discussion of many helpful responses to angry feelings, including pillow-hugging.

Step 9:

DO UNTO OTHERS

Jacob was breathless when he came home from basketball practice. "Mom, Mom! Aidan wasn't at practice today. They say his little sister died." Jacob's Mom felt sorry for Aidan and his parents. But she also was worried about Jacob. It had only been a few months since his father died and she wanted to protect her son from more grief. She thought Jacob would want to stay away from anything sad, too. So she was surprised when Jacob said he wanted to go to the wake and the funeral. "Are you sure?" she asked. "Yes, I'm sure," replied Jacob firmly. "I've been through this and I think I can help Aidan."

When Jacob's mother saw Aidan's eyes light up as Jacob approached him at the wake, she knew she'd made the right decision in letting Jacob go. She told her son that he did have something special to give Aidan. Jacob sat quietly through the funeral the next day, paying rapt attention. In a few more days, Jacob asked if they could invite Aidan over to play. The boys disappeared into Jacob's room. Jacob's mother heard the murmurs of what sounded like serious conversation and shrieks of laughter, too. That evening, Jacob told his mom that Aidan said he was an "awesome friend." Jacob looked proud and happy. His mother was amazed that her son had so much strength—and that giving support to his friend made Jacob stronger yet.

Like adults, children come to feel better about themselves when they make positive connections with others and find a way to be helpful to others. We empower our children when they realize they have something to offer.

When they are ready, encourage your children to reach out and give to others.

- This may be through a bereavement group, a social services group, a group in their house of worship, Scouts, or another organized group.

- It also may be on a more individual basis. Being a good friend to another child or being attentive to an elderly grandparent are also important ways of giving, for example.

For some children, there may be particular meaning in plunging into an activity that is related to their lost loved one.

- This could be a Walk for Cancer or playing an instrument that Mother played.

- They should not feel forced into any activity, however. It will backfire if they feel they have to do something that doesn't feel right to them.

Children should be allowed to go to funerals or memorial services of others who have meaning to them, to ask the new questions that these funerals will raise for them, and to comfort and share experiences with other children who are bereaved.

Step 10:

SEE THIS AS A LIFELONG PROCESS

Children who have been bereaved have had an experience that is life-changing. They will be different because they have experienced significant loss at an early age.

• The ways in which they may be different are often positive when they receive appropriate modeling, compassion and support.

• They can become more resilient, more empathic to others, and have a greater depth than children who haven't had to deal with death.

• They can know that they have survived through the biggest pain imaginable—they are stronger than they ever thought possible and can know in their bones that they have the resources to deal with the many challenges that anyone's life brings.

Sammy was now thirteen and a half. His adolescent mind was expanding, capable of abstract thought. And he was wrestling with some big questions as he went through the confirmation process at his church. The understanding he'd had of God and of death when he was a little boy didn't serve him anymore. He wanted to know why a just God could let a good man like his father die when so many awful people live. Fortunately, Sammy's church provided an adult mentor for youths preparing for confirmation. Sammy's mentor welcomed the opportunity to explore these issues with a teenager who took them so seriously. After months of earnest and sometimes painful discussions, Sammy reached a new equilibrium. His mother, Laura, was almost startled by his leap in maturity—which she didn't see in the same way in his friends who hadn't had to grapple with deep questions based on their own life experiences.

This is not a do-it-once-and-be-done-with-it process, however. Your children will need to grieve again and reintegrate their loss as they mature at each developmental stage.

• You can anticipate this. When it comes, don't be surprised and don't see it as a step backwards. See each re-grieving, re-working period as a necessary opportunity for growth. They often occur in adolescence, when there is a developmental leap in the capacity to think abstractly, and around anniversaries of the death or the birth date of the person who died.

• You can envision the process as like a spiral staircase, where the child may at first seem to be in the same place but is actually at a higher level.

Emma's high school graduation day was sunny and clear. Her grandparents all came, as did her favorite aunts and uncles, and, of course, her mother Laura and her younger brother Sammy. But where was Emma when it was time to take her photo with all of her proud relatives? Sammy found her behind a tree, crying softly. "Oh, Sammy, I wish Daddy could be here today. I miss him so much!" Sammy hugged his big sister and said, "I know. I don't even really remember him. But I miss him." Together, they walked back to their waiting family. To Emma's surprise, her mother guessed right away what had happened. She said she felt the same way. Her father's parents told Emma how proud her Dad would have been on this day. Emma told the gathered family how happy she was that they were all there for her. That night, she carefully put a copy of her graduation program in her old memory box, right between two pictures of her father.

- One of the disconcerting things about this process is that the need to mourn again and find a new understanding of him/herself may come at milestones which seem like they should simply be joyous occasions, such as family holidays, birthdays, graduations, first jobs, marriages, or parenthood. Know that this is normal and healthy, even though it is painful.

The next fall, when Emma went off to college, she felt a sense of purpose. She was going to follow in her father's footsteps, becoming a doctor just as he had been. But she found she didn't really like the pre-med courses all that much. And, as she really thought about it, she realized she didn't like hospitals very much, either. But how could she let go of this dream that kept her close to her father? She sought help from the college counseling service. She came to realize that she could feel connected to her father without trying to do just what he did. What they shared was their wish to help others. There were many ways to do that. She would find her own path, maybe social work.

- You and you child need to know that it is very appropriate to seek out counseling help at various times throughout your lives to facilitate the re-grieving process. This can be an ongoing process.

◆

When we talk to our children openly and honestly, answer their questions, and treat them with compassion and understanding, they will find their way through the experience of early, life-changing loss. Communication is key, acknowledging the changes in your family is essential, making time to remember feeds the soul, and patience conquers all. While it may seem impossible in the early days of grief, over time a healthy dose of the ability to laugh at ourselves helps as well.

You and your children can and will survive this experience and find your way into becoming a new family – more resilient and stronger in the broken places, moving hopefully into the future.

PARENTING CHILDREN WHO ARE GRIEVING THE LOSS OF A SIBLING

If your child has lost a sibling, you are surviving the loss of your child. This is truly a life-changing loss, upsetting both your and your surviving child's sense of safety and security. Everything can seem out of place, out of time, hazardous, and frightening. You want to reassure your child, but your own sense that things will somehow come out all right is shattered.

Certainly this is parenting at your lowest ebb, when you may feel least able to rise to the task. Looking at all the days ahead may be overwhelming. Try, as best you can, to focus on the day at hand and on what you and your child need today.

Throughout the book, the authors have counseled telling your child, "We won't always be this sad," and, after the death of your child, it may seem impossible for you to believe. But even this devastating loss is survived, every day, by families like yours. It is OK for your child to see you sad. This loss has meaning to both of you and your child knows this. Yet hope—

even the "fake it till you make it" kind—is important for your child and for you as well.

◆

Johnny was in the grocery store with his mom's friend, Debbie. He wasn't quite sure why she had taken him there, but he thought it had something to do with the commotion at the pool earlier that day. It seemed like she was just finding things to do to keep him busy and away from home.

That morning, he'd been off at the snack bar getting a popsicle and he'd waited forever because it was so hot that it seemed like the whole town had gone to the community pool. He'd heard shouts and cries of "Call 911" and he thought he heard his brother Max's name. Then Debbie hustled him off into her car as sirens started to wail. Now he'd been with her for hours. At first, Debbie just said that Mom wanted Johnny to be with her, but then, after he kept asking "Why?" she told him that Mom had to take Max to the hospital because he'd fallen into the water. Johnny was sort of worried and sort of annoyed. He'd fallen into the pool before and it wasn't a big deal. But Max was smaller, so maybe it was different. No, it couldn't be anything really bad. And now he was missing soccer practice all because of his dumb little brother.

Debbie's cell phone rang. He heard her say, "OK." She looked very white and stood very still. Debbie said that it was time to go back to his house. They drove back home without talking at all. Johnny was afraid to ask what was going on and Debbie didn't want to be the one to tell him.

When Johnny walked into the house, Mom and Dad and Grandma were sitting in the living room. There were a bunch of other people there, too, but Johnny just looked at Mom and Dad. Mom pulled Johnny against her and said, "Johnny, Max fell and drowned in the pool. He was under water too long before anyone noticed him. He breathed in water instead of air. The lifeguards tried to get the water out and the air into his body. An ambulance came and took him to the hospital, but nobody could make his body start breathing again. His body stopped working and he died." Then she cried and Dad and Grandma cried. Johnny kept repeating, "He's dead? He's dead?" but Mom and Dad just held onto him and each other. Johnny went to the room he'd shared with Max, sat on his bed and looked around. There were all of Max's toys on the shelves and his clothes in the closet. It was like this couldn't really be true.

When you tell a child about a sibling's death...

Follow the general guidelines for the surviving child's developmental level, keeping the statements simple, direct, using words and concepts the child can understand, and following the child's cues for how much to tell.

With the grief over the loss of a sibling, there often also comes a shift in the surviving children's worldview...

Be prepared for your surviving children to lose their sense of immortality, to realize much earlier than most people that even a child's life can end in death.

- This may be very hard for you because you are grappling with the sense of wrongness that comes with a child's death seeming out of the natural order of things.

- Although you may want to reassure your child that nothing else bad or difficult will ever happen to him or her, unfortunately that is unrealistic and may lead to the child's questioning your honesty or reliability.

• You can say that one of the reasons people are so sad and shocked is because the death of a child happens so rarely.

• If their sibling died of an illness that your surviving children do not have, you can state this matter-of-factly, giving them a hug and saying that you are happy they are healthy. Reassure them that they won't get the fatal illness, if this is realistic. If their sibling died from an accident or violence, realistically reassure your children about what precautions you and they can take so that this will not happen to them.

Surviving children need to have a sense of safety that comes from the confidence that their parent or parents can take care of them. You want your children to feel that they will not be alone.

• This sense of safety may have been compromised by their sibling's death.

• Speak directly to your surviving children about the things you can do to protect them and keep them safe and well.

• You demonstrate that you can take care of your surviving children by re-establishing reasonable, predictable routines for sleep, meals, getting dressed, with plenty of time for cuddling and listening.

• You can also say explicitly that you are sad and tired but you will always take care of them.

• You can reassure your child that most people die when they are older and you plan on being around for a long time.

When your children express feelings...

Be ready for ambivalent feelings about their brother or sister who died.

- If your child who died had a long illness, it's likely that he or she needed a lot of your time, attention, and energy. Brothers and sisters invested a lot of emotional energy, too.

- Let your surviving children know that sometimes children have mixed feelings—to a young child you can call this having two feelings at the same time—and that you can understand that they probably do, too.

- Let them know that they can love and miss their brother while feeling glad it's over—all at the very same time. Or love and miss him and feel mad that his illness kept you away from them. Or be jealous of all the special attention he got and guilty that they feel that way. Or love and miss their sister and feel mad that she forgot to buckle her seat belt on the day of the car crash.

If you pick up any signals of self-blame from any of your surviving children, be clear that none of them were at fault for their sibling's death.

- Some children may think, "If only I hadn't been angry at her...If only I had been nicer...She'd be alive now."

- Listen for this and let the child know that all children have mean thoughts about their sisters or brothers sometimes. Mean thoughts don't cause harm or death.

Be ready for ambivalent feelings about you.

• Sometimes, in children's eyes, their parents weren't powerful enough to keep their sibling safe, so they may be disappointed in you or mad at you. At their developmental level, they just don't really understand that some things are beyond a parent's control.

• Although the child's judgment may be unfair because it is based on a child's level of understanding rather than an adult one, try not to act defensive or angry toward him or her. That can inadvertently push the child away. Then you can get cut off from your child at a difficult time when he or she really needs you.

• You did the best you could, but you understand that it feels scary that parents can't always make things all right.

• Use words that are respectful of your child's fears and feelings, then say you're going to love him or her and take care of him or her no matter how he or she feels.

• You can tell children that they are welcome to tell you any feeling they have, but we don't scream at each other and we don't call names. Model talking about feelings in a respectful way.

When children ask how you are feeling, or use their intuitions to tell how you feel, be honest with them. Don't say you're not feeling sad when you are.

• You do not need to go into great detail about the depth of your sadness or to tell them about complicated feelings of guilt, if you have them.

• Let your children know that it's not their job to make you feel better. You won't always feel so sad.

• If there are times when you feel sad and they do not, reassure them that this is OK. People can feel different.

• While it isn't helpful to talk to your children about your complicated feelings or your very powerful feelings, it is important to find someone you can share those feelings with. This person could be someone from Compassionate Friends, a grief worker, a therapist, or member of the clergy. Start by going to compassionatefriends.org and clicking on their online support community if you feel there is no one you can reach out to in person at this time.

When you are trying to cope with arrangements in the early days, whether for the visitation, funeral, memorial service, receiving people in the home (sitting shiva for Jewish families), making notifications, handling paperwork, deciding on the gravestone…

Be ready for this to preoccupy and exhaust you. That's normal.

The day of his brother's death and the next two seemed very blurry and confusing for Johnny. The house was full of people and almost all of them brought food. Mom was crying a lot and people kept taking her out for a walk. Somebody was giving her medicine. Sometimes she would smile at Johnny and ask him how he was and he always said that he was fine. Dad was talking to people all the time and drinking beer. On the second day, Aunt Dannie and Uncle

Pete came to take Mom and Dad to the funeral home to make arrangements. Johnny had been to funerals before. He couldn't believe it was going to be Max's. After Mom and Dad came back, he asked if he could go outside. Mom said he could do what he wanted. She didn't even remember to ask where he was going or what he was going to do. Maybe Mom and Dad didn't care about him any more

On the third day, Mom asked Johnny to come into his and Max's room and they sat on Johnny's bed. She hugged him and said, "Johnny, I love you very much. I know I haven't been paying much attention to you since Max died. I've been really sad. I know it's been hard for you, too." She hugged Johnny again. "Right now there are lots of things I have to do for Max, like finish planning for the funeral. This is the only way I can take care of him now, so I need to do it. But this kind of taking care of Max will end soon and then I'll have time to pay a lot of attention to you." Johnny snuffled. "I want to take care of Max, too," he said. Mom let Johnny pick what clothes Max should wear and what he wanted to put in the casket. She felt better having this moment of closeness with Johnny and he did, too.

Explain what is happening to your surviving children, both that your attention is drawn away from them right now <u>and</u> that this preoccupation won't last forever. Do this while reassuring them that you love them and that their wish for attention is completely OK—you just can't do it all right now.

- For example: "Right now I'm talking about the gravestone and it's taking a lot of my time. It's hard because I don't have enough time to give you as much attention as you deserve. It's not always going to be like this. At some point, I won't be giving so much attention to your brother's death."

- Acknowledge that something is going on. Don't pretend that you are your usual self.

- It has to be this way right now, for this short time period.

- It can help to say something like, "You are really important to us. We know you are hurting too and we understand why you wish we could spend more time with you now. The reason it's taking so much time is because this is the end of our taking care of your brother. After this is over, we won't have to do this any more. And then we'll be able to concentrate on being your Mommy and Daddy and taking care of you."

After he'd talked to Mom for a while about the funeral plans, Johnny grew restless. "I want to go out. I want someone to play with me." Mom felt completely drained by the discussion with Johnny, even though she was glad they'd had it. "Let's go get Uncle Bob. He loves to shoot baskets." "But I want to shoot baskets with you, Mom" whined Johnny. Now that he had Mom, he didn't want to let her go. But Mom realized she had no physical or emotional energy left. "I'm glad you want to play with me, Johnny, and I'm glad you asked me. I won't always be this sad and tired. Then I'll play with you again. But right now I have to take a nap. Let's find Uncle Bob to shoot hoops with you while I rest."

Draw on other potential caretakers to give attention to your surviving children during this stressful time. It's too much to expect yourself to take care of all their needs. This is the time to let relatives, friends, and neighbors extend a helping hand. Teachers and coaches often are ready to give a little extra time and encouragement to a bereaved child or teen.

Still find some time each day to truly be with each of your surviving children. Even in your intense grief and preoccupation, you are not deserting them.

As your children grieve...

If you have more than one surviving child, remember that each of them will respond to their sibling's death in a different way.

• Each had a different relationship with their sibling who died, therefore each is mourning a different kind of loss. The hole in a child's life after having lost an admired but bossy big sister is different from the hole in his or her life after having lost a cute but pesky little sister—even if both were the same girl, just experienced from different perspectives.

• Each child is temperamentally different. One may tend to become withdrawn, while another may get hyperactive under stress. Yet another child might get weepy. Some children even deny that they cared about their sibling.

• And, of course, children of different ages will be at different stages of brain development and therefore have different levels of understanding of death and its implications.

As you start to establish new family routines...

Recognize that the family constellation has changed.

• Not only is there a missing place at the table, but your surviving child's or children's place(s) in the family change. The younger brother may become the oldest. The middle child may become the youngest. A sister may become an only child.

• This can be disorienting and upsetting for all.

• Say out loud that it feels different and let the children talk about what has changed. You and your surviving children can share feelings about the changes—that it makes you sad, confused, etc. If possible, give the children a say in some of the changes, such as the new seating arrangements at the table or the redistribution of chores.

Finally, all of the visitors who had crowded Johnny's house were gone. Even Grandma was sleeping in her own home. Johnny looked at Max's bed. No one had touched it. "Mom, how come Max's pajamas are still on his bed? He won't need them anymore. He won't even need his bed anymore!" "You're right, Johnny, he won't. But I'd like to leave them there a little longer until I get used to the idea that he won't be here anymore." Johnny found himself nodding. He, too, wasn't used to the idea that he didn't share his room with Max.

After a few more weeks, Mom asked Johnny which things of Max's he wanted to keep and which things should be put away or given away. "I want all his stuff!" Mom said he could keep it all for now, but if he decided later that he wanted more space in his room, they could talk again. The next day, Johnny presented her with an armful of Max's toys. "These are all baby toys. I don't want them. I'm just keeping the Legos and the cars." Mom took the toys Johnny said he didn't want and put them in a pile in the basement. "I'll leave them here for a while. Then, if you look again and see something you'd really like to keep, you can take it back." Sure enough, after a week Johnny retrieved his brother's favorite teddy bear as well as the plane Max used to annoy him with by buzzing his head.

Several weeks after that, Johnny announced that he wanted to make the beds back into bunk beds, the way they had been when Max was still sleeping in a crib in their parents' room. He was proud when he looked at his room after the change; it looked like a big kid's room. But that night, he came back out to the family room after his parents had tucked him in. His eyes teared as he said, "He's really not coming back, is he?"

You and your children may need a little time before changing what previously had been shared space.

- For example, if the child who died (we're calling him Max) shared a room with a sibling (Johnny), you can talk about how you'd like to leave things as they are for a little while until everyone starts to get used to the idea that Max isn't sharing the room any more.

- When you and Johnny are ready, give him a lot of say in how the room should look.

  ▶ Let him go back and forth in his decision-making if he needs to.

  ▶ This can be a way of his processing his brother's death and of establishing that he has a life of his own to lead.

- Then let the room be Johnny's room.

All of the siblings need to be a part of the decision making about what things to keep. You may be surprised by some of the things that have special meaning to them.

When you talk about the child who died...

It is important to remember the brother or sister who died as a person who was deeply loved but who was not perfect.

• Memories of the child who died tend to become elevated. While it is natural to focus on the endearing, special and cherished things about the child you lost, it can be difficult for the surviving children to compare themselves to someone who seems so perfect.

• The child who died should not become the ideal the other children cannot live up to.

▶ Try not to make comparisons.

▶ It is difficult for a child to be held up to a brother or sister who can't ever do anything else wrong or make another mistake.

• Keeping a more realistic stance about the child who died is helpful for the surviving siblings.

▶ Continue to tell stories about the brother or sister who died, but be sure they're about a real person.

▶ Tell true stories—funny ones, sad ones, difficult ones, happy ones, angry ones, proud ones, loving ones...all the stories.

If the child who died was a difficult youngster...

- It is important to acknowledge the ways in which he or she was hard to live with.

- It is also important to recall the positive things about him or her and that he or she was loved.

As you work on living in the present...

You will never forget your child who died.

- If someone asks you how many children you have, you may choose to include the child who died—"We have two children, Johnny, who is living, and Max, who died when he was five." In some situations (such as casual encounters when you don't expect to have any lasting relationship with the people you are meeting), you may decide to only name your surviving children. It's up to you to choose what feels right to you in any given situation. There is no one right or wrong way to handle this.

- But don't forget to show an interest in and tell others about what your surviving children are doing.

You honor the uniqueness of each of your children, living and dead, by valuing them for who they were and are.

- Don't expect your surviving children to fill in the gaps left by the death of their sibling.

- Sometimes surviving children will identify with the sibling who died and try to be like him/her or take his/her place. You can let them know by your words and actions that you love them each for who they are, just as you loved their sibling for him- or herself. If they genuinely share some interests, talents, or characteristics with the sibling who died, that's a piece of who they are and that's nice. But you all can remember the sibling who died without anyone trying to be him or her. No one can or should be a replacement for the mourned child.

• Everyone gets to live his or her own life.

The question that is on every surviving child's mind, in one form or another, is: Is it as important that I'm alive as it is that she's dead?

• You do not have to let go of your love for the child who died to make the answer "Yes."

• Show your surviving children that "Yes" through parenting that is loving and engaged every day.

◆

Remember to focus on the needs of you and your children each day, one day at a time. If you have the opportunity to get support as a family from a grief program in your area, we strongly urge you to give it a try. Being with others can help immeasurably. If support services for your children are not readily available, please seek support for yourself through The Compassionate Friends, a grief counselor experienced in working with grieving parents of children who have died, or any resource appropriate for you and the particular kind of loss you experienced, such as a pregnancy/infant loss group, Parents of Murdered Children, or a suicide support group.

For you and your children, hope is possible and it comes just one step at a time. The death of a child can feel like an enormous boulder that almost crushes you. Gradually, you will notice that the edges of the boulder are wearing away, almost imperceptibly at first, until it becomes a little bit smaller and a little bit lighter. After awhile, it becomes a heavy stone that is a weight on your shoulders but no longer feels absolutely crushing. After a very long time, the stone becomes small enough to put in your pocket, even though it often rubs painfully. You will always carry it with you, but you will find that even as you carry it, you can find a measure of meaning and joy in your life and, especially, in the lives of your surviving children.

PARENTING CHILDREN WHO HAVE LOST A FRIEND OR LOVED ONE TO SUICIDE

The loss of a friend or loved one to suicide can be frightening and complicated. We may even wonder if it's appropriate to tell the children what happened because we may not know how to explain it to them. If the person who died is someone you loved, chances are you're feeling confused and helpless yourself.

To begin dealing with a loss by suicide, start by keeping things simple for everybody by dealing with what you know. Understanding why and how this death occurred is long-term work and may never feel completely resolved. We can learn to acknowledge and deal with a death by suicide by beginning with the most basic facts. We can explain that depression and mental illness caused the death (which is true almost all the time). We can help our children understand that a last, desperate act does not define a person, does not make other things about the person's life a lie.

◆

Michael knew something was wrong when his mother was standing at the door to his house as soon as he got off the school bus. He was sure it was something terrible when he saw her face, which was ashen and tear-stained. As soon as they got inside the house, she hugged him. "I need to tell you about Daddy."

"What about Daddy?" Michael searched her face.

"Daddy died today." His mom started crying.

"What do you mean he died? What was wrong with Daddy?" Michael almost shouted.

"Daddy had an illness called 'depression.' "

Michael looked away, then said angrily. "What does that have to do with dying?"

"His depression made him feel so terrible and so hopeless that Daddy made his body stop working and then he died."

Michael kicked the floor and started to leave the room. Then he came back. "How did he make his body stop working?"

"He made himself stop breathing. When he couldn't breathe, his body couldn't work anymore and he died."

"How did he make himself stop breathing?"

"He used a rope."

"Oh." Michael stomped into the kitchen. "I need a snack." His mother was taken aback, but then she realized that Michael couldn't handle any more right now. He needed to do what he usually did when he came home from school—have something to eat. She poured him a glass of milk while he found the oatmeal cookies.

When you talk to your child about the death of a friend or loved one by suicide...

Your goal is to help each child form a workable narrative appropriate to his or her developmental level. This is a story that:

- makes sense to the child at his or her age and level of understanding

- is honest but does not give any more detail than necessary

- allows the child to continue loving or caring about the person who died

- does not blame anyone

- does not glamorize the death

- the child can mull over, repeat to him- or herself, and add to as needed.

Listen carefully to each child and answer the questions that child is asking, one at a time.

After he'd stuffed some cookies in his mouth, Michael looked up and burst out crying. "How could Daddy do this to us?"

His mother stroked his hair. "He didn't do this to hurt us, Michael. His brain wasn't thinking clearly."

"Mom, I don't get it."

"Sometimes people's brains get sick like a lot of other parts of bodies get sick. When that happens, the sick brains send confused thoughts and make people terribly sad, scared, and angry. When brains get sick, people can think that what's wrong now will always be wrong and can't ever change. That's a mistake: things can change. But the sick brain doesn't realize that. Sometimes when people start thinking that way, they make their bodies stop working and they die. When that happens, it's called suicide."

Michael stood up. "Mom, are you sick, too?"

His mother held him tight. "No, Michael. I am very sad right now, but I don't have a brain sickness like Daddy. I will be here to take care of you. And so will all of your grandparents."

Normalize the death by comparing this death to that of any other sometimes fatal illness. This is simply one of many forms of death. Use an explanation like that given to Michael in the vignette above.

Mute the action when discussing the death and do not go into graphic details (just as you wouldn't give graphic details of the suffering from cancer or the experience of suffocation in congestive heart failure). Keep the story as low-key and non-dramatic as possible.

• For example: "Daddy made himself stop breathing and then he died" (not "Daddy hung himself"). If the child asks a follow up question, then say, "He used a rope."

• For example: "Mommy made her heart stop beating and then she died" (not "Mommy killed herself"). "How?" "She took too many powerful pills and they kept her heart from beating."

• You want your child to learn from you or from another trusted adult that the person important to him or her died by suicide. The child will find this out from someone sooner or later, in any case. If you are the one who tells about it, you know the message hasn't been distorted and that your child can ask questions as he or she feels the need.

• Use your conversations with your child to find out what he or she imagines happened. He or she may have misconceptions that you'll need to clarify.

Focus on the illness, not the event.

• Whatever particular things happened (or didn't happen) around the time of the death, they were not the cause of death: the distorted thinking caused it.

• If focus is on the event, it is too easy for blaming to begin because somebody may think there was something that someone could have done differently. But this is always true, and most of the time it does not result in someone else ending his or her life.

• Middle school and high school students can be challenged by asking questions relevant to their situation. For example:

> ▶ "How many thousands of kids across the U.S. talked back to their mothers yesterday—and how many of those mothers took their lives?" for a middle school student worrying that he was at fault because he talked back to his mother the day she died by suicide.

> ▶ "How many parents got divorced? Did they all die by suicide?" for the high school student blaming her mother for divorcing her father, whom she just lost to suicide.

> ▶ When challenged in this way, these young people can come to the important conclusion: It was the illness, not the preceding event.

> ▶ Watch out for any signs that your adolescent is seeing suicide as an appropriate or even glamorous

way for himself or herself to deal with the stresses of life. Be clear that your adolescent can tell you if he or she is feeling a lot of pain and that he or she can get help.

• Young children are especially vulnerable to trying to make sense of the situation by seeing themselves as causing events. They need to know that their actions or thoughts did not make this death happen.

To help your child or children cope with aloneness...

Your child needs the support of all members of the extended family at this difficult time. So do you, and so do all family members. It's easy for families to get caught up in the blame game; this only tears the children further apart and makes things worse for all. (Adults who as children experienced the maternal and the paternal sides of their families becoming estranged after a suicide speak poignantly of their double loss— the person who died *and* their connection to loved family members who became distanced from them and their surviving parent or parent figure.)

• Focus on how you can be there for each other and for the children.

• Don't get involved in blaming others, and discourage others from blaming.

• Get professional help for your family if it starts to unravel.

When talking to others, such as close family friends, frame the death in a way that normalizes it as a tragedy like any other death of a parent or loved one. Be clear that this was due to illness, that no one is to blame, and that the child needs their support.

You can decide when, where, and with whom you discuss the circumstances of death.

• As people understand mental illness and suicide better, it is becoming easier to simply acknowledge the cause of death, once again focusing on the illness.

• It usually works best if you don't try to keep it a secret, while also knowing you don't need to go into it with anyone unless you want to.

▸ Then you won't have to ask your children to keep secrets or pretend. And you won't have to worry that some information will slip out sideways. Keeping a secret is difficult to do and carries the risk of children being confronted with it in intrusive ways.

▸ Remember that not keeping the circumstances of the death a secret doesn't mean you have to discuss it with everyone who asks. Just because people know doesn't mean you have to talk about it. It's fine to say, "Thank you for your interest and concern, but I don't want to talk about it" to people you don't want to have a conversation with about the death.

▸ If you're planning to disclose the cause of death, rehearse with your children what they can say both to people they'd like to really talk with and to those they'd rather not. For the first group, the child gives a simple story emphasizing the illness; for the second group, it's a version of "Thanks for your concern, but I'm not interested in talking about it."

• But this is your decision. If you choose not to disclose, be sure your children understand that you have chosen to keep details private and what exactly the sanctioned story line is. Be sure they have other avenues where they can talk freely. And be sure that no one makes a child feel guilty if he or she lets something slip out by accident.

▶ Prepare your children that even if you are telling no one outside of the family, sometimes people do find out. Help them find ways to deal with the situation if someone confronts them directly or if they overhear something.

Schools generally can be the most helpful if they know the basic circumstances of the death, framed for them as a tragic death caused by illness. Then they can be an ally for your children, helping them to navigate any social issues and making accommodations if they are needed to help a child get through the school day, such as reducing demands for assignments.

Think of whether people in other organizations your children belong to may also be more helpful resources if they know the circumstances of the death. The caring coach, the tuned-in scout leader, your clergy person and members of your faith community, and others, may be able to show extra sensitivity to your children if you give them some basic information. You be the judge of who can use such knowledge wisely.

When you talk about the person who died and your child's feelings about him or her...

Let your child see the whole person, what was lovable and what was hard to be around or understand.

It is all right for children to be angry that their loved one was so confused that he/she didn't understand that things could get better and therefore made his/her body stop living.

- Children generally can be helped over time to direct the anger at the illness leading to suicidal thoughts rather than the loved one him- or herself.

- You can review with your child what is the best thing for someone to do when that person feels his or her life should end—talk to a trusted adult and get professional help. Problems in life can be dealt with. Suicide isn't a solution, even though the person who died might have thought it was. It just leaves all those who cared about the person feeling terrible. It's not something to copy. Repeat that the person who died by suicide was ill. Reinforce that your child is a separate individual with his/her own coping skills and strength.

As you think about the positive past...

Even though the friend or loved one's death was difficult or complicated, there are still things about that person's life that the child can remember, cherish and connect with.

- The person who died had a life as well as a death and that can be remembered separately from the way he or she died.

• This positive remembering can be done through sharing stories about the person who died. Your child may want to draw pictures, write or dictate memories, and/or save keepsakes.

As you imagine the future...

Know that your children will forge their own lives and make their own choices—and help them to know that, too.

• Even if they are similar to the person who died in some ways, their lives can follow a different trajectory. Their paths will be different.

• Instead of fearing the future, focus on nurturing a resilient child.

◆

The biggest help for dealing with a death by suicide is minimizing the stigma for survivors. Explaining the death consistently as a result of a clinical illness is critical in helping you and your children understand what happened. With support and understanding, your family can integrate this loss, acknowledge the life of your loved one, remember the good things you have to remember, and walk hopefully into your future.

PARENTING CHILDREN WHO HAVE HAD MULTIPLE LOSSES

The key issue for parents and children who have suffered multiple losses is the crushing overload of loss and grief. It can feel overwhelming. It can feel as if there is no space to deal with any one of the losses because more keep piling on. It can feel as if there is nothing else going on in the world except for loss and death. That can be paralyzing. There are things you can do to keep that overload from being completely overwhelming.

◆

Chris saw her son slumped on the couch, watching TV with dull eyes. "Ben, I need to talk to you about the report from school. Your grades are slipping." "So what? It doesn't matter anyway." "Of course it matters. Ben. Good grades will help you have a good future." "Doing well in school didn't do anything for Uncle Mike," said Ben bitterly. "Or for Grandpa. Or for my friend Kevin. They were all smart and they all died anyway."

Before Chris could think of a reply, Ben spoke again. "Mom, I want a white coffin when I die." "What are you talking about, Ben?" "I didn't like Kevin's brown coffin. I want something with more class."

"Ben, we don't need to talk about your coffin. You're not about to die." "Oh, yeah. Who says? Kevin didn't think he was about to die, either, but that taxi ran him over just like that." Chris put her hand on Ben's shoulder, but he shrugged her off. "Leave me alone, Mom. You can't make me feel better."

Chris took a deep breath. "I know you really hurt now, Ben. Losing any of these important people would be hard, and losing all of them in less than two years seems like too much. No wonder you're having trouble concentrating in school. I'll call your teacher and the school social worker to let them know what you're going through." She started to say more, then stopped, because she saw that Ben could only hear a little bit at a time.

You and your children need to let grief happen...

Help your children separate the different deaths. And do so yourself.

- This honors each life and death, giving each its own integrity and meaning.

- This keeps the deaths from becoming one enormous, overwhelming mass.

- Have an image of beads on a string, each of which can be mourned and dealt with one at a time.

  ▸ They are not an unmanageable tangle.

  ▸ There is room for bits of life in between each bead.

Chris did call Ben's school. The school social worker noted that a number of students were reeling from Kevin's recent death. She was planning a short-term group for students who wanted to talk about it and also find a way to memorialize Kevin. Ben's teacher said she had no idea he'd experienced the other two deaths; she offered to give him some extra support.

Chris also shared her concerns with her ex-husband. "He's thinking that much about my brother Mike?" he asked in surprise. He knew Ben had been close to Uncle Mike when he was younger, but Ben hadn't brought his death up recently. Maybe he'd been giving off signals to his son that he didn't want to think about something painful. He'd have some man-to-man time with Ben remembering Mike—both the fun times and the irritating times they'd had with him. And they could each remind each other that they were leading different lives than the one Mike lived and that his choices weren't theirs.

In a relaxed moment when she and Ben were both feeling calm, Chris reminisced about her father and what a gift his long life had been to everyone in the family. She and Ben shared stories of going fishing with Grandpa; both the tears and the smiles that came to them felt good. Together with her sisters, they worked out a plan to have a picnic with friends and family at Grandpa's favorite fishing spot on the first anniversary of his death. Everyone could tell favorite memories, then help to scatter Grandpa's ashes in the lake.

Ben and his mother decided that every Sunday night they would light candles for each of the three important people in his life who had died. And so they did. But after about a year, Ben asked if they could cut back to just lighting a candle on the anniversary of the person's death—and a special candle for Kevin on his birthday. Chris agreed, happy that Ben was interested in other things again.

Take time yourself, and with your children, to mourn each death.

- Let each life and death have its own narrative or story that makes sense to the child.

  ▸ Each child needs to have an image of each person who died and of his or her relationship with that person.

  ▸ It is usually helpful for this to be the child's story, created by him or her with your help as needed.

  ▸ The story should be about what is important to the child, reflect the child's understanding of that person's life and death, and be accurate enough to serve as a beginning point for the child to build on.

  ▸ The child can revisit the story, add to it, or grow it as the child grows.

  ▸ Stories will vary in richness depending on the relationship the child had with the deceased. It's OK to have a fairly detailed one about someone who was central to the child's life but a rather brief or sketchy one about someone who was not as central.

  ▸ Encourage your child to include examples of his/her resilience in the narrative.

- Take time to help each child to sort out his or her feelings about each person and his/her death.

Know that you and your children do not have to comprehend the meaning of death right now. You and the children can stay focused on the individual beads, one at a time.

Let your children know that one reason this is so difficult is because it is unusual. This string of deaths is not what they can expect for the rest of their lives.

Recognize that children can be overwhelmed by multiple losses that come within a short time frame, even if each one in itself might not be too much if it were the only one. If this happens to your child, follow the same script of separating the losses, helping the child to deal with them one by one. (See Appendix B for an illustrative example.)

When you set priorities...

Know that you and your children may not be able to—or need to—devote equal amounts of attention and time to each loss situation.

It may happen that the loss which is most important to you is not the loss which is most important to your children. Each person in your family will probably be impacted differently by different losses because every relationship is different.

  • For example, a family of four could have been buffeted by four separate losses, each of which was devastating to one member of the family but did not tear a hole in the lives of the other family members.

▶ The death of the maternal grandmother who lived in a distant state and was visited rarely might have a deep impact on the mother (her daughter), but cause less disruptive sadness for her husband and the children.

▶ The loss of the father's business partner could profoundly affect him, but barely register with the children.

▶ The death of her close friend might mean the most to one of the children, while the death of the long-time babysitter might be most important of all to another child.

• For you as the parent, this means respecting each child's perspective when dealing with that child. It may be challenging to see the altered landscape from his or her point of view because it can be so different from your own, but it will feel good to both of you when you can feel that empathy.

• Recognize the importance of the loss as it impacts your child. When you do, you won't inadvertently belittle his or her loss and won't expect him or her to share your perspective.

• Give yourself space and time to do your own grieving understanding that each person will do this differently—you and your other family members won't mirror each other.

Pay attention to the physical needs of you and your children, such as sleep, exercise, and stress-reducing activities. Attention to these needs isn't selfish; it's essential.

Identify activities that fill you up rather than drain more energy. Then talk with and observe your children to figure out what is energy-boosting for them. Pick and choose which activities feel good to them. Don't expect them to be able to keep on with an overscheduled life if they had one before.

Find as many resources as you can...

Be sure to let key members of the staff at their schools know that your children have experienced a lot of losses.

• Work with the principal or other appropriate personnel to find supports for your children in school. A teacher to whom your child is close, a school counselor or social worker, or a nurse may give your sad and overwhelmed child a place to grieve and lower his/her stress level.

▸ Your child may feel that the stimulation in the classroom is just too much at times. Then he or she needs a break to close his/her eyes and breathe deeply. A child often signals this need by having some physical complaint so that he or she can go to the nurse. It is important that the teacher and the nurse know that this means the child needs a short "time out."

▸ Often the child and the teacher can work out a special signal for this "time out" so that the child doesn't have to come up with physical symptoms. They also can work out a place for the child to go when this happens. Often this is the nurse's office, but sometimes it is the social worker or counselor's office, or with support personnel, such as an aide or an administrative assistant. The title doesn't matter if it is a person with whom the child feels safe and comfortable.

• You may need to advocate for some leniency in homework load and for the opportunity to redo tests during times of great stress.

Don't always turn to the same people for support.

It's easy to fall into relying on just a few wonderful friends or family members who have stuck by you and your children through all the stress. Value these people and continue to give them important places in your lives, but be careful that you don't burn them out.

Think of how to broaden the network of caring people who can provide support, companionship, and mentoring to your child—and to you.

• Add to your list of friends, relatives, scoutmasters, coaches, youth leaders, etc.

• Remember that one person doesn't have to be able to—and probably can't—do everything.

• Look for different people to provide different parts of what is needed.

Consider professional help from a grief worker or group, or a psychotherapist if your child becomes so overwhelmed that he or she seems seriously depressed or is functioning very poorly for a period of time.

When you all feel tense and stressed out...

Try doing relaxation exercises, such as deep breathing and "Rainbow Relax" with your children (see page 52).

Do other fun· physical activities like bike riding or swimming together. Some families have "dance night" when they put on music and dance in whatever wild or silly way they feel like moving.

When you and your children talk about the past and the losses it contains...

Help your child see that it's not really about him/her. It's simply what happened. And say to yourself that it's not really about you, either. You and your children happened to be in the fallout zone.

You can be very empathetic to the sense of pain and burden your child feels while still working to help frame this situation as losses that can be dealt with one at a time. Each loss stands on its own and is not a reflection on your child, on you, or on your family.

When you examine the future...

Monitor yourself to be sure you're not focusing on the negative future.

While it may seem that only bad things ever happen, past losses do not necessarily predict future losses. And dwelling on their possibility definitely keeps us from appreciating the people and the good things in our lives now.

Watch out for signs that your child assumes the future will inevitably bring nothing but more losses. Some children may assume that all these losses mean their own death will come in the near future.

- With some children, concrete examples of probability may help them grasp that because something has happened two or three times in a row, that doesn't mean it will happen again. You can throw a die, see what number comes up first, then see how often it comes up. It won't be every time as the child might think. If initially the child's number comes up a lot, keep on throwing and let probability do its work.

- If the child starts to talk about a negative future, say: "Let's think of some other endings, too. How else could the story (or story of your life) go?"

- Consider professional help if your child cannot shake his or her conviction that his or her—or your—life will end badly or soon.

Encourage your children's hopes and dreams for the future. Have them draw pictures or write stories. Put them on the refrigerator or the wall.

When you examine the present...

Focus first on noticing small things that are positive or at least neutral. It may be too hard for your child to think in any kind of big picture.

• You can use the beads on a string metaphor for yourself and your adolescent children. What was the string—the aspects of life that were not death-related—today?

• For little children, simply notice and enjoy with them the pleasant or fun things that happen. Say them out loud.

It's really important to help your child see all the many ways in which he/she has been and continues to be resilient.

• Write note cards each night about a moment when your child did something hard, new, or emotionally strong. Or put this onto the computer, smart phone or notepad. This draws attention to your child's resilience in the face of repeated adversity. This needs to become part of his/her self-image.

• Notice, document, and pat yourself on the back for all the ways you have been and continue to be resilient, too. You are getting through challenging times.

Give your family lots of warm, restorative time together.

• During this time, have no particular agenda other than to enjoy each other and the present moment.

• "Family" can mean just you and one child, or any other combination of parent, parents, or parenting figures plus child or children that fits your situation.

• This can be the time for activities done with each other, such as talking, playing board or card games, reading, baking, watching DVDs, shooting baskets, biking...anything you all can enjoy doing at the same time. Let the children help choose what to do.

• Include grandparents or other family members sometimes if they are close to you and your children.

You and your children can start to see yourselves in new ways...

The first step is to see yourselves as survivors of these losses, not victims.

Next, challenge yourself and your children to notice what else each of you are, beyond the being the survivors of these losses. What is there if that identity is not on center stage?

• Notice things your child does, talents he or she may have. For example, your child may be a soccer player, an artist, a computer whiz, or be good with the dog.

• Notice positive personal characteristics. Your child may also be a good friend, a good sport, someone who tries hard even when homework is difficult, or have a fun sense of humor.

• You can play a game in which each of you writes two positive things about yourself and two things about each of the other family members present.

As your children become less shell shocked, encourage them to gradually expand their horizons to include new activities and interests if their lives seem to have become too narrow. But stay alert to the danger of over-programming.

Older children and adolescents may need to grapple with big questions about the meaning of life and death.

• Your job isn't to answer these questions for them. Just be their sounding board.

• It is fine to encourage them to talk about these issues with someone from their place of worship, a wise and trusted teacher, or another mentor.

Remember that dealing with and eventually overcoming the grief of multiple losses is a process...

Don't get discouraged if feelings of depletion, sadness, anger, or being overwhelmed don't disappear easily. The goal is to have these feelings gradually diminish and, more often than not, be replaced by a sense that you and your children live in a NOW that has value.

Expect mini relapses and see them as part of the process. These relapses don't mean that you or your children are going backwards.

Also expect your children to need to re-work their understanding of their losses as they progress to new developmental levels. True for all loss experiences, this is particularly the case for multiple losses.

◆

Anticipate that you will have interesting, complex children with capacities for resilience they otherwise might not have developed. They can grow into adults you will be happy to know.

PARENTING CHILDREN WHOSE FRIEND OR LOVED ONE WAS KILLED BY ANOTHER PERSON

It is always difficult to learn that a person important to you and your children was killed by another person. Yet it is important to know that such deaths can take many forms. Exactly how you talk to your children about the death of a loved one who has been killed by another person will depend in part on the specifics of this particular death...

◆

The cause of death of the child's friend or loved one may have been *murder*, or it may have been labeled something else such as *manslaughter*, or the death may have been the consequence of an automobile crash when someone else was at fault.

- The death may have taken place in public or in private.

• The person may have been killed intentionally or unintentionally.

• The killer may have known the victim or never seen the victim before.

• The death may have been the result of a face-to-face encounter or one in which the victim never saw the person who killed him or her.

• The person important to your child may have been the only victim or one of several victims.

• The victim may have been engaging in some activity that was illegal or dangerous (although there almost always could have been an outcome other than homicide) or the victim may have simply been minding his or her own business.

• The person who killed your child's loved one may have clearly been seriously mentally ill or may have appeared to be coldly rational.

• The death may have occurred someplace out of your child's neighborhood or it may have happened close by.

• Your child may even have witnessed the event or the aftermath. (If so, please look at the next section on trauma.)

Painful as it is, you want to get the facts straight so that you can tell the children what happened or help them to understand what happened.

When you talk to the children about their friend or loved one's death...

Give this death time and space boundaries, explaining when, where, and how it happened.

Tell about the death in a way that does the least damage to the child's sense of safety. By telling about it as something that happened in a particular place at a particular time, you help the child keep it limited rather than fanning fears that it could happen to anybody anywhere.

Very often, the circumstances were the reason that this death happened. Frequently, there was no planning or forethought.

Don't emphasize the action when discussing the death and do not go into graphic details (just as you wouldn't give graphic details of the suffering from cancer or the experience of suffocation in congestive heart failure). Reduce the drama.

- Example: "There was a fight. The person made Daddy stop breathing and then Daddy died." To the question "How?", respond, "He used a knife."

- Example: "Grandma was in her car, stopped at a traffic light. The driver of the car behind her wasn't paying attention and was driving much too fast. We have traffic signs to tell people how to drive, but he broke the rules. Most drivers do not. Instead of stopping, that driver crashed his car into grandma's car and completely smashed it. Grandma's heart stopped beating and then she died."

- Example: "A man was shooting his gun. He was careless. One of the bullets hit your sister and made her stop breathing and then she died."

- Example: "There was a lady whose brain was very sick. She got very confused and thought other people were trying to hurt her, even though they weren't. She made some of those other people stop breathing and then they died. One of them was your uncle." How? "She used a gun."

Talk to your child about what precautions you are going to take, how you are going to protect yourself and your child.

While you can talk briefly about the person whose actions killed your child's friend or loved one, it isn't helpful to try to give deep explanations of why he/she did it or of his/her psychology. Focus on what the person did. That is what caused the death.

- If it is clear that the person who killed was severely mentally ill, it is a good idea to include this in the explanation. Don't use this explanation if it isn't true, however.

- Talk about a person who did harmful things, dangerous things, or careless things that hurt others, rather than about a "bad person" or "bad people." When children just hear about "bad people," it can add to their nervousness and fear because they can start to think that the world is full of bad people and that they or those they love might be victims at any time.

Listen carefully to your child and answer the questions your child is asking, one at a time.

Don't tell the child more than he or she wants to know, but be sure to clear up any misconceptions. Sometimes what children imagine happened is worse or more frightening than what actually happened.

- Be sure that your child is clear that he or she is not responsible for the death. Children are especially vulnerable to trying to make sense of the situation by seeing themselves as causing events to happen. They need to know that their actions or thoughts did not make this death happen and that it was not their responsibility or within their control to prevent the death.

- Be sure that the child or adolescent does not feel responsible for avenging the death ("getting back" at the person who killed his or her loved one). Children and adolescents need to know that revenge is unacceptable. It does not honor their loved one and will result in more harm, risk, and violence.

Your goal is to help each child form a workable narrative or story about this death appropriate to his or her developmental level.

- A workable narrative is a story that makes sense to the child at his or her level of understanding, is honest but does not give any more detail than necessary, and allows the child to continue loving or caring about the person who died. This is a story that the child can mull over, repeat to him- or herself, and add to as needed.

- This story should be about this death as a unique event that has a place and a time specific to it.

- First, you'll want to know what the child is imagining or thinks happened so that you can help him/her understand what actually happened.

- As much as you can, frame the story in a way that lets the child feel as safe as possible.

  ▶ Usually this means helping the child separate his or her situation from that of the victim.

  ▶ Part of the story is what you do to keep the child safe from dangerous circumstances.

  ▶ You can matter-of-factly tell what the next steps are going to be. For example: "The police will work to find the person who killed your cousin, (if that has not yet happened). Once the perpetrator is found, there will be a trial. After someone is found guilty, that person is punished, usually by being put in jail. (The person responsible for a fatal car crash may get a lighter sentence; if so, your family will deal with this together.) This process will take time, but we as a family will go on living our lives day by day while this all happens. And there will always be someone to take care of you."

To help your child (or children) cope with aloneness...

Your child needs the support of all members of the extended family and community at this difficult time, and so do you, and so do all people affected by this death. It's easy for those grieving the loss of the person who was killed to get caught up in the blame game and the intricacies and legal ramifications; this only tears the children further apart and makes things worse for all.

• Focus on how you can be there for each other and for the children.

• Hold the person or people who were responsible for the fatal act accountable for what they did. Assign responsibility and consequences where they belong (the person who pulled the trigger or the person who drove drunk and dangerously, for example), but don't let blaming spill over to everybody who knew anything or might have done something differently. That kind of blaming leads to separation and division instead of coming together in the face of tragedy. And coming together is what is needed.

• Get professional help for your family if it starts to unravel.

Help your children figure out who they are comfortable talking with about this death and what they are comfortable sharing. They may want to tell one or two trusted people almost everything, others just the basic facts, and not talk about it at all with others.

• Death by homicide or in a car crash is generally public information and cannot be kept private, but you don't have to talk about it at any length with everyone. Rehearse with your children what they can say in different situations, including when they'd rather not talk about it. For example, "Thank you for your interest and concern, but I don't feel like talking about it."

• Shield your children from T.V. and newspaper reporters and photographers who want to ask them questions or take their pictures. Worrying about what to say to an interviewer (or getting comments from others about what he or she has said to the media) adds stress at an already stressful time. You may want to choose a spokesperson to deal with the media—an adult relative or a clergyperson, for example.

• It is appropriate to talk to your children about what makes them comfortable. As much as possible, give them some control over who is going to talk to the school and how they would like the school to tell other students about the death of their loved one.

Think about what communities you and your children are a part of. Which ones can provide a sense of comfort, caring, and belonging?

• Caring communities could include your church, synagogue, or mosque; your children's schools; your neighborhood; your child's boys' or girls' club; a bereavement group for children; or a victim support group, to give some examples. If the victim was one of your children, you can connect with other parents going through similar pain through Mothers Against Drunk Driving or Parents of Murdered Children, as applicable.

▶ While it is nice when the whole family can be supported by the same community, sometimes it happens that a connection that is extremely important to one family member is not as important to another.

Schools can be helpful in supporting students whose loved one was killed by another person.

• The school can be your partner in helping your child through difficult days. Be sure that the school knows about your child's loss.

• Classrooms of students can be prepared by a counselor or social worker to be respectful of your child's desire to talk or not to talk about the death. Children can be encouraged to show support, but told that a lot of talking, rehashing, or gossiping about the death creates drama instead of promoting a supportive atmosphere.

• A teacher to whom your child is close, a school counselor or social worker, or a nurse may give your sad (and maybe angry and/or frightened) child a place to vent and to grieve.

▶ Your child may feel overwhelmed by the stimulation in the classroom at times and just need a break to close his or her eyes and breathe deeply. A child often signals this need for a break from the overwhelming stress by having some physical complaint so that he or she can go to the nurse. The teacher and the nurse need to know that the child needs a short "time out."

▶ Often the child and the teacher can work out a special signal for this "time out" so that the child doesn't have to come up with physical symptoms. They also can work out a place for the child to go when this happens. Often this is the nurse's office, but sometimes it is the social worker or counselor's office, or with support personnel, such as an aide or an administrative assistant. The title doesn't matter if it is a person the child feels safe and comfortable with.

• If the death was one that affected many students, encourage the school to have trained leaders hold group gatherings to help the students work through their feelings, to remember the person or people who were killed, and perhaps do a memorial display.

You may want to look for victim support groups and victim advocacy groups where your child can gain from being with others going through the same kind of experience and have access to professionals who know how to be helpful to them.

When you talk about the person who was killed and your child's feelings about him or her...

Let your child see the person who died as a whole person, both what was lovable and what was hard to be around or understand. But let the child focus on those aspects of his/her loved one that were positive and likeable.

If the person who was killed put him- or herself in a dangerous situation, that can be acknowledged without blaming the victim.

• You can talk about the victim not having been careful enough or having made a poor decision to be in a particular place at a particular time.

• Be clear that the person who killed the loved one made a bad decision, did something harmful, did something dangerous, or did something careless. Almost always, the person who killed made a bad choice and that resulted in the loved one's death.

When you deal with your child's feelings about this death...

It's normal to feel completely worn down after losing someone to violence. The whole experience is exhausting for your mind, body, and spirit. Don't expect you or your children to have a lot of energy right after this death. Give yourselves extra rest and be sure you're eating well and exercising. Tone down expectations for a while. But check the next section on trauma to learn how to recognize when you or they may need extra help.

Children who have lost someone because of someone else's actions often have a lot of anger and a lot of fear. You may, too. If you expect this, you can help your child (and yourself) manage these feelings. You can channel these feelings in ways that will be helpful rather than increasing the sense of being overwhelmed, helpless, or fearful.

For both anger and fear, there are short-term techniques you can use to help keep your child from being overwhelmed in the moment. And there are longer-term actions you and your child can take to direct your energies in a useful way.

For anger:

- If your child is angry at any particular moment in a way that interferes with his or her daily functioning—can't concentrate on homework, explodes at Grandma for something unimportant, hits the dog, for example—work with him/her to deal with anger in a better way.

▶ It often helps to begin by a simple, empathetic sound like "Unh," followed by simple words— "Sounds like you're really hurting." This helps the child feel that you're connecting with his/her pain and he/she is not alone.

▶ Most very angry children need a next step of either cooling down through stepping back and breathing deeply or working off their hot energy in constructive ways like exercise. See page 68 for some specific anger management techniques.

▶ If the child has done or is threatening to do something violent, dangerous, or mean, be completely clear that he/she can always tell you about angry feelings, but he/she must use words. It is never OK to hurt someone or an animal, and it's not OK to hurt himself or herself either.

▶ The goal is for the child to be able to put anger into words. At first those words are likely to be about something on the surface, like not being able to get the shoes he/she wants or the way Grandma sings when she cooks. You can listen sympathetically and say you're sorry he/she feels that way.

▶ Then watch for opportunities to talk about the anger under the surface—the sense of injustice, helplessness, fear, and sadness that comes when someone we care about is killed by another person. Knowing he/she is not alone, that you understand, what you are doing to keep him/her as safe as possible, and that his/her anger can be channeled toward the real problem of irresponsible driving or violence all do help.

• To help your child—and yourself—deal with the "bigger picture" anger:

▶ Channel the anger toward a cause. Join with others, if you can.

— Neighbors can work together to push for stop signs at unsafe intersections to help prevent others from being killed by motor vehicles. They can also work with the police for better enforcement of traffic laws. You can join Mothers Against Drunk Drivers to keep drunk drivers off the streets.

— There are already-established groups that work to prevent gun violence and to ensure that the mentally ill receive adequate care and do not have access to weapons. You can join them. Some have ways that children can become involved.

— Local city officials and/or police can respond to pressure for safer parks and streets, after-school programs, and jobs programs. Churches can help. Parents can ask that students not have to cross from one gang territory to another (or that they are adequately protected if they do).

Neighbors can band together to "take back the streets" from drug dealers and gang members.

▶ Help your child to see that making something of his or her life is the best response against violence. He or she doesn't have to allow the perpetrator to make him or her a second victim.

▶ Anger at the individual(s) responsible for the death of your child's loved one may remain. This is normal. While forgiveness may eventually feel freeing, it usually doesn't come quickly and it's not for everyone. The best outcome for your child and for you is not to be crippled by anger.

For fear:

• Do what you realistically can to keep you and your children safe and tell your children what you are doing. Your focus will depend on the nature of the death your family experienced and the dangers your children may face.

• Go over safety rules for riding in the car (and driving it, if you have teenagers) including the use of seatbelts. Review how to cross streets safely as a pedestrian.

• Work with the school to be sure there is adequate security in school and on the way to and from school, if this has been an issue. Be sure your children know safety rules for the street.

• Work with the school to develop and enforce a strong anti-bullying program.

• Discuss the safety precautions you take at and around home. Rehearse with your child what to do in potentially dangerous situations.

• Let your children know who to get hold of in an emergency and how to do so.

> ▶ If there can be a network of people who care about your child and will keep their eyes open for him or her, that is wonderful.

> ▶ Tell your children that if they can't reach someone they know but feel unsafe, they can turn to a police officer, school personnel, or a mother to get help.

• If your neighborhood is basically a safe one, let your children have as much independence and responsibility as is appropriate for their age within the safety rules you set. They need to learn how to get along in the world and it is hard to do that if they spend all their time locked up in the house or apartment. Can they walk to school in a group? Is there a supervised after-school program or playground where they can get some exercise?

• If your neighborhood or surrounding area is unsafe at this time, you can band with others to try to get after school programs and other safe places for children to play. Until you are successful in getting a program or if you cannot get one, find ways for your children to exercise their minds and bodies at home. Highlight and talk about places where you can maintain safety: How you keep your own home safe, how grandma's block is safe, how your church is safe, for example.

• If your child is full of exaggerated or unrealistic fears, look at pages 47 through 51 of this book and see the steps for dealing with anxiety. The work you've done in making the story of the loved one's death very specific will be useful here. (Appendix A has an example of how parents can explain anxiety to their children. You can adapt the story to fit your specific situation.)

> ▶ You can say to your child that the *Mr. Worry* part of his/her brain is trying to convince your child that his/her situation is the same as the situation of the person who was killed. But it isn't and you can tell *Mr. Worry* how it is different.

> ▶ In addition, your child can argue with *Mr. Worry* by telling him of all the ways your family is keeping itself safe.

• Larger picture activities, such as working with neighbors, churches, schools, and/or the police to make the neighborhood safer are also important ways to channel the anxiety you and your children may feel into something that helps make things safer for all. So does working with established organizations for the causes that have become important.

• If your child shows ongoing signs of re-experiencing the trauma, he or she may have what is called Post-Traumatic Stress Disorder (PTSD). See the next section, **A Few Words about Trauma.**

As you think about the positive past...

Even though the friend or loved one's death was difficult or complicated, there are still things about that person's life that the child can remember, cherish and connect with.

- The person who died had a life as well as a death and that can be remembered separately from the way he or she died.

- This positive remembering can be done through sharing stories about the person who died. Your child may want to draw pictures, write or dictate memories, and/or save keepsakes.

As you imagine the future...

When you talk and act like your children can have a positive future, you help your children feel that they will have a life and it will be worth living.

Know that your children will forge their own lives and make their own choices—and help them to know that, too.

- Even if they are similar in some ways to the person who was killed, their lives can follow a different trajectory, a different path.

- Instead of fearing the future, focus on nurturing a resilient child.

Seek help if you want or need it...

Notice what is going on with your children. While you expect some anger, fear, general anxiety, and separation anxiety, ordinarily these will gradually recede as time passes.

• If one or more of these (anger, fear, general anxiety, and separation anxiety) keeps getting worse instead of better…

• If one or more of these compromises the child's ability to learn, play, or sleep…

• If one or more of these makes it much harder for the child to interact or relate with others, if he or she is having a much harder time getting along with others than he or she used to…

• Then ask for professional help.

• You can also check the next section in this book, **A Few Words about Trauma**, to see if your child may be suffering from traumatic stress. Full-blown Post-Traumatic Stress Disorder needs professional intervention from someone trained in dealing with it.

Asking for help isn't a way of saying that there is something seriously wrong with your child or that you aren't a good enough parent. It's a way of being a good parent by getting help for your child before problems get so big that they interfere with your child growing up to be the most he or she can be.

And know that it is OK to ask for help for yourself. You may be overwhelmed by everything that's happened, both the death itself and the demands made on you to keep on going, keep on parenting. That's understandable. You deserve support and counsel if you want it.

◆

Helen Keller once said, *"Although the world is full of suffering, it is also full of the overcoming of it."* You and your children are more resilient than you may know today. With attention, support, effort, and justice, hope is possible.

A FEW WORDS ABOUT TRAUMA

Some of the children whose parents or caretakers are reading this book may have had traumatic experiences associated with the death they are grieving. The difficult job of helping them through their grief (and you through yours) becomes even more complicated. This section can help you figure out whether your child may have experienced trauma, give you some ideas for helping your him or her shortly after the event, and assist you in deciding whether you or your child need the help of a trauma specialist.

The words *trauma* and *traumatic* are often used loosely to refer to any tragic or difficult experience that happens. The death of someone who is very important to a child almost always is difficult and tragic, but usually it is not traumatic, because trauma has its own special meaning and trauma is different from grief.

Although there are a number of different kinds of events that can be traumatic, those most likely to have affected grieving children are:

- Violent acts that result in serious injury or death

- Serious accidents

- Natural disasters

- Witnessing any of the above

Traumatic events usually contain one or more of the following conditions:

- They directly threaten the life or bodily integrity of the child or are perceived by the child as threatening in this drastic way

- The child has witnessed an act of violence or mutilating injury or grotesque death, heard unanswered screams for help or cries of pain, or was near an act of violence

- The child experienced being trapped or without assistance or feeling helpless in an extreme situation

The level of trauma escalates when the incident was one of deliberate human design. The damage that one person can do to another leads to the most traumatic experiences. Thus natural disasters tend to be less traumatic that witnessing or experiencing brutal violence.[7] However, what is traumatic is different for every person, so someone else's experience may be different from your child's. And your child's experience may be different from your own.

If you feel your child may have experienced trauma

1. **Establish or re-establish safety.** Be sure your child is physically secure from any further threats and tend to any physical injuries or shock.

---

[7] R. Pynoos, A. Steinberg, and A. Goenjian "Traumatic Stress in Childhood and Adolescence," Traumatic Stress, edited by Bessel A. van der Kolk, et al., pp. 336-337.

2. Give the child an opportunity to tell about the event, but don't insist on a child talking right away if he or she doesn't want to.

a. Some children need to talk about the event very soon afterward in order to understand fully that it is over.

b. Other children need to wait until they have been strengthened by some or all of steps 3 through 7 before they are ready to tell in detail what happened.

c. Follow the child's lead and respond to his or her need to tell his or her story.

d. Be careful not to grill the child. Ask only questions that help to get it straight. These are "Who, what, where, when" questions that have specific and factual answers.

e. Identify the time and place of the event. It happened there and then. This helps to keep it limited to a particular incident or incidents rather than letting the event seem like a model of how life is in general.

f. You aren't seeking to provide a grand explanation of why these things happen or why people can act that way. You are simply looking to have a story you and the child can use to recount the event.

g. You can ask how the child felt then and how he or she feels now, what the hardest part was and how he/she got through it. This can become part of the story that the child tells.

3. Let your child know that you and the other adults will work toward solutions. Examples of solutions for two different post-trauma situations are:

a. After an act of violence, having the perpetrator put in jail

b. After a disaster, finding safe temporary shelter and then re-building a more secure house (or finding a new one)

4. Re-establish routines. Get the child back into a normal rhythm of existence. Having a sense of predictability is important.

5. Keep the child connected to others. A sense of isolation makes trauma worse, while feeling like a part of a caring group of family members, community members, peers, and/or fellow survivors reduces negative effects of trauma.

6. Encourage the child to actively help others and to do constructive things. Acts of mastery reduce the sense of helplessness that is a hallmark of trauma, give the child some sense of control, and further connections to other people.

7. Help your child to see him- or herself as a person who can actively make things better. This can reduce the negative impact of trauma.[8]

a. These actions can be on a small, immediate scale, such as reading to a younger child who is also suffering or helping to pick out household items that are still usable after a flood.

[8] For discussion of suggestions 1 and 3-7, see B. van der Kolk, A. Mc Farlane, and O. van der Hart, "A General Approach to Treatment of Posttraumatic Stress Disorder " in B. van der Kolk et al., *Traumatic Stress* p.425.

b. Or they can be on a bigger scale, such as joining a neighborhood rally against violence.

8. Give hope that this event won't occur again or to this child. It was limited and it is over with, even though you all still have strong feelings about it. Again, reassure the child as to the steps adults are taking to prevent this from happening again. Listen to your child's specific worries and deal with them one at a time.

✓

9. Expect your child—and yourself—to have less energy than usual for a while. Trauma is exhausting. It takes time to recover.

Trauma is different from grief, though children may experience both trauma and grief as a result of the same incident.

In grief, the overwhelming emotion is sadness.
In trauma, it is terror.

The pain associated with grief is pain of loss.
The pain associated *with terror is powerlessness and a feeling of being in jeopardy.*

When children draw pictures of themselves in grief, they often draw themselves crying and/or looking sad.
When traumatized children draw themselves, they often draw themselves as disfigured.

Fantasies, daydreams and dreams of grieving children often center on the person who died.
In traumatized children's dreams and fantasies, the dreamer often becomes the victim.

— 141 —

When grieving children show anger, they are often oppositional. *Traumatized children often show their anger by being aggressive and impulsive.*[9]

Children can experience trauma and have a reaction to it without developing full-blown Post-Traumatic Stress Disorder (PTSD).

• If the child has experienced trauma that is not moving into PTSD, trauma symptoms will gradually lessen and be noticeably less problematic after 4 to 6 weeks.

• If symptoms keep getting worse and/or persist after 6 weeks, seek professional help from someone trained in dealing with PTSD.

• These symptoms include:

  ▶ Re-experiencing the trauma

    – **Flashbacks:** Feeling as though he or she is back in the event—"I'm there again!" The child may stare into space as he/she goes back into the experience.

    – **Intrusive thoughts and images:** Troubling images that pop into the child's mind—bits and pieces from the event. The child could be playing, then suddenly get an image of the person's bleeding head.

[9] Core Course, "Children of Trauma," given by William Steele, PsyD., Director of The National Institute for Trauma and Loss in Children, 2001.

– **Traumatic dreams:** Nightmares in which the child or someone he/she cares about is in harm's way.

– **Physiological reactions:** Restlessness, ringing or roaring in ears, a dropping sensation in the abdomen, exaggerated startle responses.

- **Avoidance**

  ▸ **Dissociative behavior:** Feeling like he/she is someone other than his/her real self and is watching what happens to the real self as if from a distance.

  ▸ **Detachment and Disconnection:** Lack of eye contact, resistance to being touched, diminished response to people when these symptoms had not been characteristic of the child before. You have the sense that the child is not responding to you.

  ▸ **Avoidance of things connected to the traumatic event:** Not wanting to be near a person—even a victim— or near places associated with the traumatic event.

  ▸ **Flat affect:** Not having any strong feelings or responses, diminished interest in things he/she used to care about.

  ▸ **Play that seems pressured:** The child has to repeat things over and over without gaining any sense of mastery or satisfaction; obsessive-compulsive-like play.

> ▶ **Phobic behaviors:** Being scared or terrified of certain things or places.

• **Arousal**

> ▶ **Cognitive dysfunction:** Inability to focus or recall; inability to process verbal information. The child has trouble making sense of what others are saying.

> ▶ **Hypervigilance:** Being over-alert to possible dangers; hiding behind piles of pillows and under blankets at night, or sleeping behind furniture, for example. "Hiding sleeping"—sleeping in another room where the child is not expected to be.

> ▶ **Startle responses to noises that ordinarily wouldn't faze the child**

> ▶ **Fear of separation from parent or caregiver**

> ▶ **Irritability, aggressiveness, assaultiveness**

Children who have these symptoms need treatment for Post-Traumatic Stress Disorder (PTSD). This specialized treatment will help them deal with the trauma. PTSD is not something that normally goes away on its own. Treatment early on helps to keep it from interfering with the child's life or going underground and popping up in painful and unexpected ways later on.

They will still have grief responses that must be dealt with. The grief process still needs to happen for these children. Working through the trauma is an important first step, but that alone is not enough. The general information on grieving children as well as the specifics for different types of death given in this book should be very useful in helping them with their grief.

Remember to take good care of yourself as the caregiver of your children. You also may need additional help for traumatic stress or PTSD as well as your own grief. You need to be sure to get yourself what you need both because you are important in your own right and because your children need you.

AFTERWORD

Twenty-two years old and a recent college graduate, Angela is a very poised, self-assured young woman, with a ready and empathetic smile for every grieving child who crosses her path at the bereavement group she once attended and now volunteers for. For all who know her, Angela is the walking, talking evidence that significant, life-changing loss does not ruin a child's life. It can change the path of children's lives dramatically and, like every other life-changing experience, it does not leave them as it found them. Because of her experience, Angela has become someone different than she might have been. And that someone is a person with incredible compassion, depth, honesty, and a commitment to making a life that means something... for herself and in honor of her brother as well.

As Angela talks about the death of her 12-year-old brother when she was 15, she looks wistful and vulnerable. She shares her thoughts about a relationship that meant, and continues to mean, the world to her. Remembering the moment of her brother's death, she says, "I'm not happy I was there for it or sad that I was there for it. But it's a memory I'm glad I will always have."

She smiles just a little bit. "It was good to be with him. The last thing he ever said to me is that he loved me and the last thing I said to him was that I loved him too. I'm glad I was there to let him go. He's always with me in my heart. I take him wherever I go."

It's never easy to lose someone important to you through death, whether you are a child or an adult. Sometimes we wish with all our hearts that the children and teens who are dear to us would never have to experience such a loss. But many do. We can't keep them from feeling pain. We can, however, help to keep that pain from overwhelming them by being there for them, letting them know that they are loved, their concerns are heard, and their emotions are understandable. We can answer their questions honestly without giving them more information than they can handle at that time. We can help them hold sustaining memories of their loved ones, and see themselves as resilient and resourceful. They can come to realize that if they lived through this, they can live through whatever comes their way in life. We can encourage an attitude of living each day as it comes, finding something in it to appreciate. We can support their natural push toward growth and find joy in their hopes and dreams. We can nurture their belief that they have something important to offer to other people, that the pain they have felt can be a source of empathy. We can give these children our hands as they move forward in their meaningful lives.

APPENDIX A

A Story about Anxiety—Managing It Step by Step

Isabel was very close to her grandmother, who lived nearby. Until recently, Isabel would go over to her after school until her parents came home from work, preferring that to the after school care program at her school. A broken hip sent Grandma to a nursing facility, but Isabel visited her every week. Isabel was off at overnight camp with the Girl Scouts when her grandmother got pneumonia and became seriously ill. She died peacefully shortly after Isabel was rushed back from camp to say "Good-bye" to her. Isabel initially was caught up in all the preparations for the funeral and held her composure during the service. She appeared to be listening to her parents when they explained that Grandma was old, that her body had been weakened by the broken hip, and that pneumonia was a common and often fatal illness for elderly people in her condition.

Isabel's parents understood when she didn't want to go back to camp for the remainder of the session. But they became concerned when Isabel didn't want to leave the house to play with friends at their homes. She turned down an invitation to her best friend's birthday party, saying she had a stomachache. When Isabel's mother, Amy, tried to insist, Isabel froze on the sidewalk in front of her friend's house, turning pale, breathing rapidly, and then sobbing. Amy had to take her home.

Her parents sought advice about how to help Isabel. Following the suggestion of an experienced counselor, Amy told Isabel a story:

"Back in the days when there were cavemen and cavewomen, there were lots of dangers. There were poisonous snakes and saber tooth tigers and other animals hanging around that could kill people—people had to react very quickly to get out of the way.

"Sometimes cave people got mixed up about why things happened. They thought that because two things occurred at about the same time that meant one caused the other. Even though they really didn't have anything to do with each other. Like if someone died while they were out of the cave, they thought that being out of the cave was dangerous and caused the death.

"We all have a part of our brain that reacts right away to anything that seems like it might be dangerous. There is a fancy name for it, but I'm going to call this part of the brain Mr. Worry. Mr. Worry sends signals to our bodies that get us tensed up for action in response to the danger we think we see. Some people call this the 'fight or flight' response. This all happens before we have had a chance to use the part of our brain that thinks things through carefully to figure out whether there really is something to be scared about. It's like our cave person brain—our Mr. Worry—acts before our 21st Century thinking brain has a chance.

"Unfortunately, Mr. Worry likes to make dangers seem bigger than they really are, to see threats in situations that are only a little bit like something which actually could hurt us, and to believe that because two things happened at about the same time, one thing caused the other. Like when one cave person got sick and died when the other one was away. Those two things really didn't have anything to do with each other, but Mr. Worry tries to make us think that they do. And Mr. Worry doesn't know how good we can be at getting through the tough time.

"Mr. Worry was useful in cavemen days when it was best to act very fast to avoid anything that could possibly be dangerous and he's

useful in extreme moments of real danger today, like when you need to jump out of the way of a car that's coming at you. But for most 21ˢᵗ Century situations, this quick response makes things worse for us. We tend to tense up and avoid the things that make us anxious without ever using our smart 21ˢᵗ Century thinking brains to think carefully about these situations and how to handle them. When Mr. Worry takes over, we're like the caveman running away from a stick without ever taking time to see that it's a stick not a snake. And sometimes we stay away from the place where the stick was so we never find out that it was just a stick. Or we just keep on feeling we can't leave the cave area without ever finding out that Grandma's illness wasn't caused by us being gone."

Isabel had been paying close attention, but she started to get squirmy. Her mom said they could keep talking another time.

That evening, Isabel asked why Mr. Worry made things worse. Her mom answered, "He tries to tell us to stay away from anything that makes us feel worried or scared. But if we do that, we never find out three important things:

"First, sometimes—lots of the time—Mr. Worry has got it wrong.

"Second, the high level of uncomfortable feelings in our bodies (those stomachaches, the fast breathing and fast heart beat) will gradually go down after about 10-15 minutes if we just hang in there.

"And third, there are ways to cope with challenging situations if we do it bit by manageable bit."

"So what do we do?" asked Isabel.

"You and I can work together to keep Mr. Worry from taking over and keeping you from doing what you want to do," her mom replied. "I used the name Mr. Worry, but would you like to make up your own name?"

They played around with different names, with Isabel considering Mrs. Make-It-Worse and Scare Dragon before deciding on <u>Mrs. Worry</u>. Amy felt that Isabel had done enough for one day.

The next day, she and Isabel made up some note cards. On one side they wrote what Mrs. Worry was trying to make Isabel believe. Isabel came up with these words on her own. (As she wrote them down, Amy realized that her bright, capable daughter really was being pestered by mistaken ideas that her absence had caused Grandma's death and that if Isabel was away from her parents, they could die, too.) On the other side of each note card, they wrote why Mrs. Worry was wrong, using the words Isabel could say to talk back to Mrs. Worry. On Mrs. Worry's side: "Grandma died because I was away." On Isabel's side: "Grandma was old and frail and got very sick. She didn't die because I was away. She died because she was frail and sick." On Mrs. Worry's side: "Something terrible will happen to Mom and Dad if I leave them." On Isabel's side: "Mom and Dad are healthy young adults. They go to work and come home again every day. They are fine when I'm out of the house." Amy also taught Isabel how to breathe deeply from her diaphragm when she started to get anxious feelings.

With Amy's support, Isabel listed all of the things she was afraid to do in order of scariness. At the top was the hardest—to go back to camp. At the bottom—scary but maybe not impossible—was to go out with Dad and a friend, leaving Mom alone in the house. They practiced what Mrs. Worry was likely to say to Isabel when she did this and what Isabel would say back to her. Then she and Dad tried going for ice cream without Mom. Isabel was frightened, but she did her deep breathing, talked back to Mrs. Worry and found that her anxiety lessened enough to manage the outing. Her parents told her that she was brave. A few days later, they tried the next challenge on this list, Amy taking Isabel to her best friend's house to play for an hour. Gradually over the next several months, they worked up the list, giving Isabel sincere congratulations each time she took the next small step and praising her efforts even when she wasn't successful in meeting a challenge the first time she tried. They also helped Isabel compile a recipe book of all the favorite dishes that Grandma made as a way to foster lasting happy, comforting memories. By the time the Girl Scouts had a winter overnight outing for Presidents' Day weekend, Isabel was able to go, after rehearsing what she would do if Mrs. Worry tried to reappear.

APPENDIX B

A Story about Many Small Losses Adding Up to a Big Burden

Erin's mother, Jennifer, was concerned about her. Normally an upbeat, energetic 8-year-old girl, recently Erin had become whiny and often complained of being tired. She stared off into space and sighed heavily several times a day. Erin sometimes cried when her mother went to leave the house. Jennifer talked to some of her friends at church. They told her that another little girl with similar symptoms had been helped by a local bereavement program for children. Jennifer was skeptical—that child had lost her father and no one in Erin's immediate family had died. Still, she realized, there had been a number of losses in Erin's world that could have affected her. Could she possibly be grieving those losses? Jennifer decided it wouldn't hurt to explore this possibility.

Jennifer listed all the losses the family had experienced in the past few months when she sat down with a facilitator at the bereavement program. Jennifer's great-aunt had died. While Erin had little relationship with this elderly relative, Jennifer had been very close to her great-aunt, who was like a grandmother to her, and had been surprised by the depths of her own grief. An older neighbor who had babysat for Erin when she was little died while Jennifer was still mourning her great-aunt. Then Erin's pet rabbit had died. And there was the father of that family from church, whose daughter Erin knew from Sunday school.

The facilitator and Jennifer began to talk about each death separately, trying to sort out what each individual loss meant to Erin. Jennifer realized that her own grief over her great-aunt's death could have affected Erin and also have made her less available to her daughter. The neighbor/babysitter was someone Erin was close to at one time and Erin still saw her as part of her "safety net" of people who could take care of her. Losing a beloved pet is hard for most of us and simply getting a new one doesn't make us forget the one we lost. Even though Erin did not know the father of her Sunday school classmate well, the idea that a parent could die was scary and Erin had been moved by the sadness she'd seen in the bereaved girl's face. The facilitator explained to Jennifer that any one of these losses on its own probably would not have been overwhelming for Erin. But experienced together in a relatively short space of time, "There are just too many rocks in Erin's basket." They decided that Erin would benefit from joining a bereavement group made up of children her own age while her mother got parental guidance.

Over the next few months, both in the bereavement group and at home, the adults in Erin's life began to help her separate the different events and talk about each death on its own. Taking cues from Erin, Jennifer focused on different things when discussing each death. When they talked about Jennifer's great-aunt, she told her daughter, "I think it was hard for you to see me feeling so sad. But I know that my great-aunt lived a wonderful long life. I am feeling better and I don't think I'll be really sad very much longer. That's what it's like when someone dies—you feel sad, then you feel less sad, and then you feel better. And I know that I need to pay attention to your feelings, too, and I'm doing that now."

When they talked about their neighbor/babysitter, they remembered together all the fun things she and Erin did together and thought about how Erin could hold on to those memories.

When they talked about the rabbit, Jennifer was startled to learn that Erin worried that she hadn't cared for her bunny well enough and that was why Snowflake died. She told Erin that rabbits don't live anywhere near as long as people and that Snowflake had just come to the end of a long life. "And you can love your new bunny Fluffy and miss Snowflake, all at the very same time."

Finally, Erin shared her concerns about her Sunday school classmate whose father had died. In her bereavement group, Erin saw that it was very hard for children whose parents die, but she also saw that her classmate and other children in the group were doing OK. Sometimes they were sad and sometimes just like their old selves. Jennifer could say to her daughter that both she and her husband were very healthy. It was just Mr. Worry who was trying to tell Erin that they could have cancer like her friend's dad. (See pages 47-51.)

The things that had seemed so snarled up together didn't seem so overwhelming to Erin (or her mother) anymore. One by one, Erin had gotten to know and understand something about each "rock" in her basket. Then she could find a way to carry some along and leave others behind as she moved forward in her own grieving and growing.

References

Cain, Jack and Anne Hatcher Berenberg, Ph.D. *NOW: Overcoming Crushing Grief by Living in the Present*. Winnetka: JJC Publications, 2009.

Chansky, Tamar. *Freeing Your Child from Anxiety*. New York: Broadway Books, 2004.

Chansky, Tamar. *Freeing Your Child from Negative Thinking*. Cambridge: Da Capo Press, 2008.

Huebner, Dawn. *What to Do When Your Temper Flares*. Washington, D.C.: Magination Press, 2008.

Van der Kolk, Bessel A., Alexander C. McFarlane and Lars Weisawth, editors. *Traumatic Stress: The Effects of Overwhelming Experience on Mind, Body, and Society*. New York: The Guildford Press, 1996.

Additional Helpful Resources for Parents

Fitzgerald, Helen. *The Grieving Child: A Parent's Guide*. New York: Fireside, 1992.

Fitzgerald, Helen. *The Grieving Teen: A Guide for Teenagers and Their Friends*. New York: Fireside, 2000.

Grollman, Earl. *Talking About Death: A Dialogue between Parent and Child*. Boston: Beacon Press, 2011.

Horsley, Dr. Gloria and Dr. Heidi Horsley. *Open to Hope: Inspirational Stories of Healing After Loss*. Palo Alto: Open to Hope Foundation, 2011.

Johnson, Joy and Marv. *Children Grieve, Too*. Omaha: Centering Corporation, 2008.

Smith, Harold Ivan. *When A Child You Love is Grieving*. Boston: Beacon Hill, 2004.

Steele, William, *Helping Your Child Conquer His/Her Fears*, The National Institute for Trauma and Loss in Children. www.starrtraining.org/tlc (for trauma).

www.dougy.org (for information on bereavement centers).

ACKNOWLEDGEMENTS

We are grateful to many people who helped us to make this book what it is.

This book began to take form after Joy Johnson, co-founder of the Centering Corporation, urged Anne to write a companion to our book *Now: Overcoming Crushing Grief by Living in the Present* especially for parents of grieving children and those who have taken on a parenting role. She encouraged us to write about the special circumstances selected. And she made many helpful editorial suggestions after reading an early draft, showing a special sensitivity to the parents' perspective.

We were able to be more articulate about the issues faced by children who have experienced the death of a loved one by suicide and how parenting figures can help because of our discussions with Bruce Engle, M.S.W., then Program Director at LOSS (Loving Outreach to Survivors of Suicide), a program of the Catholic Charities of the Archdiocese of Chicago.

Thomas Nagy, Ph.D., drew on his long experience as a clinical psychologist to help us sharpen our early ideas and to assure us that this would be a useful contribution to both families and professionals.

Alexandra Harrison, M.D. and Lisa Cohen, M.A., each brought their expertise in working with children and parents to bear on their helpful comments.

Rabbi Earl Grollman, the author of so many helpful books about grief, has been wonderfully supportive. It was he who suggested that we include illustrative vignettes to more vividly ground our words in the everyday experience of our readers.

Judith Feigon Schiffman, M.S.W., Director of Barr-Harris Children's Grief Center in Chicago, has enthusiastically and generously given of her time to read several drafts of this book, making thoughtful comments each time.

Lorna Romano worked with us to copyedit the book while keeping it reader-friendly. She did so with warmth, flexibility, and commitment to the goals of the book, as well as with skill.

Many other colleagues and friends have enriched us with their wisdom over the years...too many to mention by name, but we deeply appreciate them all.

We would like to thank our families for their loving support. Our children, in particular, are the inspiration for this book.

And most importantly, we would like to thank the many children, adolescents, parents, grandparents, aunts, uncles, teachers, and others who care for grieving children whom we have had the privilege to know and work with over the years. We have learned so much from you about grief and about love, empathy, resilience, strength, and hope.

ABOUT THE AUTHORS

Anne Hatcher Berenberg, Ph.D., draws from personal and professional experience when she writes about parenting grieving children. Anne has a B.A. in Social Relations from Harvard University, an M.A. in Psychology from Boston University, and a Ph.D. in Clinical Psychology from City University of New York. Anne was widowed when her two children were young, parenting them as they coped with the death of their father, then of their grandmother, and then of their 8-year-old friend in a school shooting. Formerly Director of Psychology at the Josselyn Center for Mental Health in Northfield, Illinois, Anne now has a private practice in Northfield where she sees children, adolescents, and their parents. Reach her by emailing anne@grieving-children.com.

Photograph by Jack Cain

Vicki Scalzitti, Manager of Children's Bereavement Services for Rainbow Hospice and Palliative Care, Mount Prospect, Illinois, began journeying with bereaved families after the accidental drowning of her five year-old son Joey. Since 1990, she has worked with grieving children and adults, offering consultation, support groups, and family camps. Vicki is an accredited school crisis/trauma specialist; she provides support to school communities during and after critical incidents and develops educational programming for school personnel. She is a workshop presenter for The Compassionate Friends local chapters and national conferences. Vicki is writing *A Year of Good Mourning*, a manual and activities guide for children and family bereavement programming. vicki@grieving-children.com.

*Photograph by
A Sterling Design*

Jack Cain has written 4 books, including *Now: Overcoming Crushing Grief by Living in the Present* (co-authored by Anne Hatcher Berenberg). The survivor of 3 deaths in his family within a 20 month period–his son, his wife, and one of his daughters–he has also written articles on grief that have appeared in several publications. Currently, he is finishing *Max and M.B.*, a book for middle grade children, and working on a new book of fiction for young adults. Jack and Anne were married in 2009. jack@grieving-children.com.

Photograph by Robert Hatcher.

Anne and Jack are contributors to *Open to Hope: Inspirational Stories of Healing After Loss* by Drs. Gloria and Heidi Horsley.